LUCY KIRKWOOD

Lucy Kirkwood is a playwright and screenwriter. Her plays include *Tinderbox* (Bush Theatre), *Hedda* (Gate Theatre), *Beauty and the Beast* and *Mosquitoes* (National Theatre), *NSFW*, *The Children*, *Maryland* and *Rapture/That Is Not Who I Am* (Royal Court), and *it felt empty when the heart went at first but it is alright now* (Arcola Theatre). *Chimerica* premiered at the Almeida Theatre in 2013 and transferred to the West End, winning Best New Play at the Olivier and Evening Standard Awards, as well as the Critics' Circle and Susan Smith Blackburn Award. *The Children* premiered at the Royal Court in 2016 and opened on Broadway at Manhattan Theatre Club in 2017. It was the winner of the Writers' Guild Best Play Award and nominated for a Tony Award. Most recently she has written the book and co-written the lyrics for the musical adaptation of Roald Dahl's *The Witches* at the National Theatre. Her screen work includes *Adult Material* and *Foreign Skies* (Channel 4) and *Maryland* (BBC2).

Other Titles in this Series

Mike Bartlett
THE 47TH
ALBION
BULL
GAME
AN INTERVENTION
KING CHARLES III
MIKE BARTLETT PLAYS: TWO
MRS DELGADO
SCANDALTOWN
SNOWFLAKE
VASSA *after* Gorky
WILD

Chris Bush
THE ASSASSINATION OF KATIE HOPKINS
THE CHANGING ROOM
CHRIS BUSH PLAYS: ONE
FAUSTUS: THAT DAMNED WOMAN
HUNGRY
JANE EYRE *after* Brontë
THE LAST NOËL
ROCK/PAPER/SCISSORS
STANDING AT THE SKY'S EDGE
   with Richard Hawley
STEEL

Jez Butterworth
THE FERRYMAN
THE HILLS OF CALIFORNIA
JERUSALEM
JEZ BUTTERWORTH PLAYS: ONE
JEZ BUTTERWORTH PLAYS: TWO
MOJO
THE NIGHT HERON
PARLOUR SONG
THE RIVER
THE WINTERLING

Caryl Churchill
BLUE HEART
CHURCHILL PLAYS: THREE
CHURCHILL PLAYS: FOUR
CHURCHILL PLAYS: FIVE
CHURCHILL: SHORTS
CLOUD NINE
DING DONG THE WICKED
A DREAM PLAY *after* Strindberg
DRUNK ENOUGH TO SAY I LOVE YOU?
ESCAPED ALONE
FAR AWAY
GLASS. KILL. BLUEBEARD'S FRIENDS. IMP.
HERE WE GO
HOTEL
ICECREAM
LIGHT SHINING IN
   BUCKINGHAMSHIRE
LOVE AND INFORMATION
MAD FOREST
A NUMBER
PIGS AND DOGS
SEVEN JEWISH CHILDREN
THE SKRIKER
THIS IS A CHAIR
THYESTES *after* Seneca
TRAPS
WHAT IF IF ONLY

Lucy Kirkwood
BEAUTY AND THE BEAST
   with Katie Mitchell
BLOODY WIMMIN
THE CHILDREN
CHIMERICA
HEDDA *after* Ibsen
THE HUMAN BODY
IT FELT EMPTY WHEN THE HEART
   WENT AT FIRST BUT IT IS
   ALRIGHT NOW
LUCY KIRKWOOD PLAYS: ONE
MOSQUITOES
NSFW
RAPTURE
TINDERBOX
THE WELKIN

Winsome Pinnock
LEAVE TAKING
ROCKETS AND BLUE LIGHTS
TAKEN
TITUBA

Stef Smith
ENOUGH
GIRL IN THE MACHINE
HUMAN ANIMALS
NORA : A DOLL'S HOUSE
REMOTE
SWALLOW

Jack Thorne
2ND MAY 1997
AFTER LIFE
BUNNY
BURYING YOUR BROTHER IN
   THE PAVEMENT
A CHRISTMAS CAROL *after* Dickens
THE END OF HISTORY…
HOPE
JACK THORNE PLAYS: ONE
JACK THORNE PLAYS: TWO
JUNKYARD
LET THE RIGHT ONE IN
   after John Ajvide Lindqvist
THE MOTIVE AND THE CUE
MYDIDAE
THE SOLID LIFE OF SUGAR WATER
STACY & FANNY AND FAGGOT
WHEN YOU CURE ME
WHEN WINSTON WENT TO WAR WITH
   THE WIRELESS
WOYZECK *after* Büchner

debbie tucker green
BORN BAD
DEBBIE TUCKER GREEN PLAYS: ONE
DIRTY BUTTERFLY
EAR FOR EYE
HANG
NUT
A PROFOUNDLY AFFECTIONATE,
   PASSIONATE DEVOTION TO
   SOMEONE (– *NOUN*)
RANDOM
STONING MARY
TRADE & GENERATIONS
TRUTH AND RECONCILIATION

Lucy Kirkwood

THE HUMAN BODY

NICK HERN BOOKS
London
www.nickhernbooks.co.uk

A Nick Hern Book

The Human Body first published in Great Britain as a paperback original in 2024 by Nick Hern Books Limited, The Glasshouse, 49a Goldhawk Road, London W12 8QP

The Human Body copyright © 2024 Lucy Kirkwood

Lucy Kirkwood has asserted her right to be identified as the author of this work

Cover artwork by AKA

Charles Chaplin's final speech from *The Great Dictator* copyright © Roy Export S.A.S. All rights reserved

Typeset by Nick Hern Books, London
Printed in Great Britain by Mimeo Ltd, Huntingdon, Cambridgeshire PE29 6XX

A CIP catalogue record for this book is available from the British Library

ISBN 978 1 83904 326 0

CAUTION All rights whatsoever in this play are strictly reserved. Requests to reproduce the text in whole or in part should be addressed to the publisher.

Amateur Performing Rights Applications for performance, including readings and excerpts, by amateurs in English should be addressed to the Performing Rights Manager, Nick Hern Books, The Glasshouse, 49a Goldhawk Road, London W12 8QP, *tel* +44 (0)20 8749 4953, *email* rights@nickhernbooks.co.uk, except as follows:

Australia: ORiGiN Theatrical, *email* enquiries@originmusic.com.au, *web* www.origintheatrical.com.au

New Zealand: Play Bureau, 20 Rua Street, Mangapapa, Gisborne, 4010, *tel* +64 21 258 3998, *email* info@playbureau.com

USA and Canada: Casarotto Ramsay and Associates Ltd, see details below

Professional Performing Rights Applications for performance by professionals in any medium and in any language throughout the world should be addressed to Casarotto Ramsay and Associates Ltd, *email* rights@casarotto.co.uk, www.casarotto.co.uk

No performance of any kind may be given unless a licence has been obtained. Applications should be made before rehearsals begin. Publication of this play does not necessarily indicate its availability for amateur performance.

www.nickhernbooks.co.uk/environmental-policy

The Human Body was first performed at the Donmar Warehouse, London, on 16 February 2024. The cast was as follows:

IRIS ELCOCK	Keeley Hawes
GEORGE BLYTHE	Jack Davenport
BOB DANVERS-WALKER / GRAHAM HAWES / JULIAN ELCOCK / MR SIEVES / DUNCAN / DUSTMAN / WAITER / REYNOLDS / MR FLACK / AMERICAN REPORTER / USHER	Tom Goodman-Hill
HELEN MACKESON MP / MRS HOWELLS / MRS ARBUTHNOT / SHIRLEY / MR CLEGG / WAITRESS	Siobhán Redmond
INTERVIEWER / GLADYS / JEAN / MRS SIEVES / MARION CUTLER / SYLVIA SAMUELS / JUDY / MRS THWAITE / MR JESSUP / ERICA / AVERILL HUGHES	Pearl Mackie
LAURA ELCOCK / BARBARA SIEVES	Flora Jacoby Richardson and Audrey Kattan

Directors	Michael Longhurst and Ann Yee
Designer	Fly Davis
Lighting Designer	Joshua Pharo
Sound Designers and Composers	Ben and Max Ringham
Video Designers	Nathan Amzi and Joe Ransom
Associate Designer	Tom Paris
Associate Video Designer	Owen Visser

Fight Director	Bret Yount
Intimacy Director	Sara Green
Voice Coach	Barbara Houseman
Dialect Coach	Penny Dyer
Dialect Coach	Hazel Holder
Casting Director	Anna Cooper CDG
Production Manager	Chris Hay
Costume Supervisor	Lisa Aitken
Props Supervisor	Martha Mamo for Propworks
Props Assistant	Lauren Thompson for Propworks
Wigs, Hair and Make-up Supervisor	Suzanne Scotcher
Wigs, Hair and Make-up Manager	Rhona Phipps-Tyndall
Wigs, Hair and Make-up Assistant	Dani Michalski
Dresser	Katie Flynn
Resident Assistant Director	Grace Duggan
Rehearsal Company Stage Manager	Lizzie Donaghy
Company Manager	Kate McDowell
Stage Manager	Daniel Haynes
Deputy Stage Manager	Katie Stephen
Assistant Stage Manager	Edie Fitt-Martin
Technical Assistant Stage Manager	Antonia Howlett
Camera Operator	Jack Somerset
Automation Operator	Matt Neubauer
Sound No. 1	El Theodorou
Assistant Set and Costume Designer	Rimu Kwok
Assistant Lighting Designer	Cheng Keng
Assistant Sound Designer	José Guillermo Puello
Stage Management Intern	Joshua Sparks
Production Photographer	Marc Brenner

For Fran B, Ruth G, Ciara M and James T

Acknowledgements

I would like to thank the following people for their invaluable contributions to the development of the play: Ed Hime, Michael Longhurst, Ann Yee, Craig Gilbert, Keeley Hawes, Jack Davenport, Tom Goodman-Hill, Siobhán Redmond, Pearl Mackie, Tessa Ross and Mel Kenyon.

This play was inspired by and heavily draws on David Kynaston's brilliant social history, *Austerity Britain, 1945–1951*.

Other sources which have been invaluable include: *The Citadel* by A. J. Cronin, *Welcome Home* by Ben Wicks, *Edith Summerskill: The Life and Times of a Pioneering Feminist Labour MP* by Mary Honeyball, *Red Ellen: The Life of Ellen Wilkinson, Socialist, Feminist, Internationalist* by Laura Beers, *Jennie Lee: A Life* by Patricia Hollis, *Alice in Westminster: The Political Life of Alice Bacon* by Rachel Reeves, the vast treasure trove of Pathé films available on YouTube, the account by Roald Dahl of Patricia Neal's stroke and rehabilitation in the Australian *Women's Weekly* (22 September 1965), Dr Geoffrey Rivett's extraordinarily detailed online document, *1948–1957: Establishing the National Health Service*, and *Homecoming: Voices of the Windrush Generation* by Colin Grant.

L.K.

Characters

in order of appearance

BOB DANVERS-WALKER
DIRECTOR
IRIS ELCOCK
LAURA
HELEN MACKESON MP
INTERVIEWER
GLADYS
GRAHAM HAWES MP
OFFICE GIRL
GEORGE BLYTHE
JULIAN ELCOCK
WAITRESS
JUDY STOPES
MRS HOWELLS
MRS ARBUTHNOT
SYLVIA SAMUELS
AMERICAN REPORTER
MR SIEVES
BARBARA
ERICA
SHIRLEY RYAN
DUNCAN RYAN
DUSTMAN
WAITER
USHER
REYNOLDS
JEAN
MRS THWAITE
MR FLACK
MR JESSUP
MR CLEGG
GIRL
WINSTON CHURCHILL

MRS SIEVES
MR EAVIS
MARION CUTLER
HOTEL MANAGER
AVERILL HUGHES

Suggested Doubling

1. IRIS ELCOCK
2. GEORGE BLYTHE
3. LAURA / BARBARA / GIRL
4. BOB DANVERS-WALKER / GRAHAM HAWES MP / JULIAN / AMERICAN REPORTER / MR SIEVES / DUNCAN RYAN / DUSTMAN / WAITER / REYNOLDS / MR EAVIS / MR FLACK
5. HELEN MACKESON MP / WAITRESS / MRS HOWELLS / MRS ARBUTHNOT / SHIRLEY RYAN / WINSTON CHURCHILL / HOTEL MANAGER / MR CLEGG
6. DIRECTOR / INTERVIEWER / OFFICE GIRL / GLADYS / ERICA / JEAN / MRS SIEVES / MARION CUTLER / SYLVIA SAMUELS / JUDY STOPES / MRS THWAITE / MR JESSUP / AVERILL HUGHES

Setting

Act One takes place in January 1948, in Shropshire and London.

Act Two takes place between May and July 1948, in Shropshire, Blackpool and Wales.

Notes on the Text

Although the scenes are set across multiple locations, a fluid, economical style of staging should be found. Please don't be weighed down by slavish detailed realism.

This play must be produced in a sustainable manner.

An asterisk (*) before a line indicates simultaneous speech.

A forward slash (/) indicates an overlap in speech.

A comma on its own line (,) indicates a beat. A beat is shorter than a pause. It can also denote a shift in thought or energy.

This text went to press before the end of rehearsals and so may differ slightly from the play as performed.

Prologue

BOB DANVERS-WALKER, *a British Pathé film announcer, enters. Muffler round his neck. Scripts in his hand. There is a mic.*

BOB. Morning, gang.

We hear the DIRECTOR*'s voice through a speaker.*

DIRECTOR (*voice-over*). With you in just a tick, Bob.

BOB. All right. You want to kick off with the war in Palestine or the Lady Doctor?

Pause.

DIRECTOR (*voice-over*). The Lady Doctor.

BOB. Jolly good. (*Very sotto.*) Doctor, Mrs, Councillor, Doctor, Mrs, Councillor –

He dissolves into coughing.

I'm so sorry, I've got the most stinking cold. I'll be all right in a – (*Another cough.*) excuse me. I'll be all right in a minute.

He takes out a hip flask, a medicinal swig. That's better.

DIRECTOR (*voice-over*). All right, shall we go for one?

BOB. Certainly.

He speaks into the mic. A live-action portrayal of a Pathé newsreel begins.

Doctor, Mrs, Councillor. A Pathé close-up of Iris Elcock.

IRIS ELCOCK (*late forties*) *enters, posing with her twelve-year-old daughter* LAURA.

One of the busiest women in England, Mrs Iris Elcock, takes time off for a stroll with her daughter, Laura. But she can't afford to relax for long! Soon she's off to work, as Doctor Elcock, GP.

LAURA *skips off.* IRIS *picks up her doctor's bag.*

One of the sick and suffering will soon be feeling better for her quiet sympathy and skill in the art of healing.

IRIS *swaps her doctor's bag for a shopping basket.*

And when Doctor Elcock has finished her morning rounds, she takes on her second job of the day, as a housewife, though like all mothers, her coupon situation won't always let her buy just what she wants.

IRIS *swaps her basket for a briefcase.*

Time now to set off on her *third* job, to Westminster, for Doctor Elcock is also Labour Councillor for South Shropshire, and Parliamentary Secretary to Miss Helen Mackeson MP, one of Mr Bevan's advisers in the Ministry of Health.

HELEN MACKESON MP *enters (sixties, red hair, Leeds accent) in a fug of cigarette smoke, and shakes hands with* IRIS *for the camera.*

Together they are part of the team hoping to implement the National Health Service Act later this year, to make healthcare available to all, free of charge. Here in the Lady Members' room, Doctor Elcock and Miss Mackeson, known as 'the Fiery Particle', discuss a speech on malnutrition.

He starts coughing again.

Excuse me.

He exits, as HELEN *steps up to the dispatch box in the House of Commons Chamber.*

HELEN.... The Right Honourable Gentleman has said that there is no need for a welfare state, as there are more deaths in this country from overfeeding than underfeeding. I think he must be speaking of his own acquaintances and not from a knowledge of the country at large. Are we to –

Parliamentary laughter from the MPs.

Thank you, are we to understand that –

Lights up on IRIS, *listening to a feed of* HELEN*'s voice coming through a speaker, she mouths the speech along with her.*

IRIS *and* HELEN. – it is the considered view of His Majesty's Government that the working classes of this country cannot allow themselves to hope for a better standard of health than the one they presently tolerate?

A female INTERVIEWER (*twenties*) *enters.* IRIS *sits with her, a little stiff.*

BOB. As you can see, Doctor Elcock isn't afraid to face tough questions. And here's a young housewife who isn't afraid to ask them.

INTERVIEWER. Doctor Elcock, are you dismayed by the threat to the National Health Service presented by the opposition of so many members of your own profession?

IRIS. Well of course we can't do it without them! It's really a revolution, what we're attempting, and nobody enjoys change – I know I don't! But the people cannot wait any longer.

INTERVIEWER. And tell me, do you think many women could live a double existence as you do? Earn their living outside of the home and still bring up their families?

IRIS. Oh certainly. But only if the community helps them. We need day nurseries, like the ones which worked so well during the war. And of course the other thing is that you must have a cooperative husband!

They both laugh.

It doesn't work at all if the husband objects! But I've got one of those so I'm very lucky.

INTERVIEWER. He's a doctor too, is that correct?

IRIS. Yes, Julian's a GP.

INTERVIEWER. But not an MP!

She laughs.

IRIS. Well, neither am I, yet!

INTERVIEWER. Yet!

IRIS. Indeed.

A lull. Eventually:

INTERVIEWER. Do you have any household hints or tips for the viewers at home?

Pause. IRIS fixes her with a benign smile.

IRIS. To keep a lettuce fresh, place it in cold water with a small, clean lump of coal.

INTERVIEWER. Thank you.

Pause. IRIS looks at camera. A shift in her, less sugar, more grit.

IRIS. Was that all right?

DIRECTOR (*offstage*). Yes, thank you, Doctor Elcock, we're just checking the gate.

IRIS looks at her watch.

ACT ONE

One

January 1948. The House of Commons ladies' lavatory. As IRIS *enters,* HELEN *is wearing a loud zebra-pattern coat and going through papers with* GLADYS, *her secretary.*

IRIS (*the coat*). Where on earth did you find that?

HELEN. Dickins and Jones. It's marvellous, isn't it? How did it go?

IRIS. I sounded a bloody fool, should never have let you talk me into it.

HELEN. Do you want to become an MP or not?

IRIS. Yes of course. / But –

HELEN. Well you must do these things if you want to reach the women's vote –

IRIS. Helen, I've written five articles in the past month alone to appeal to the women's vote, / don't –

Interrupting, HELEN *turns to* GLADYS.

HELEN. Gladys, do you read the *Workers' Weekly*? *Tribune*? *The New Statesman*?

GLADYS. No, ma'am, I read *Good Housekeeping*, sign here please.

HELEN *looks at* IRIS – *'See?' – and signs the papers* GLADYS *proffers.*

IRIS. Are you on the ten o'clock? I thought we might go over the research on dentistry –

HELEN. No, I'm in the London flat tonight. Here, powder your nose before you go.

ACT ONE   17

She hands IRIS *a compact. Gives* GLADYS *a look.*
GLADYS understands, retreats.

IRIS. I – all right…

IRIS *checks her face, powders her nose.*

HELEN. You shouldn't be so self-conscious. You're very articulate, you know, if only you could stop being so clenched.

IRIS. Clenched?

HELEN. Yes. It makes it seem as if you're trying to give us medicine we don't want. When actually, Socialism is inevitable.

IRIS *laughs, returns the compact to* HELEN, *who checks her own face.*

The country voted for it didn't they? It was all there in the manifesto, 'Labour is a Socialist party, and proud of it.'

IRIS. That was three years ago. The country isn't drunk on victory any more, it's poor and bored and tired and one day the window for change – real change I mean – will close. It's already closing. Very soon it will be shut, and we shan't be able to get it open again.

HELEN. What an intoxicating ray of sunshine you are. While we're on our own. Don't you think you'd better speak to Julian?

IRIS. What do you mean?

HELEN. You know what I mean.

IRIS *laughs at her solemn face.*

IRIS. Helen, I honestly do not have the foggiest idea.

And now HELEN *is on the back foot.*

HELEN. Iris, he's been speaking out against the Health Service.

Pause. IRIS *stares at* HELEN, *trying to conceal her horror.*

My God. You really didn't know, did you? Iris –

IRIS. I think. No, I. There must be a mistake, Julian and I are very much... he feels / as strongly as I do that –

HELEN. He's put himself forward to represent the 'No's at the BMA meeting.

A long pause, IRIS *reels.* HELEN *takes out a letter. Hands it to* IRIS.

This came across my desk. He's sent it to at least a hundred consultants and GPs in the west of England.

IRIS (*reading, sotto*). 'No promises the minister may make in the press are worth a tinker's cuss.'

HELEN. Yes, it's rather fruity. Obviously something like this... looks rather bad for us. For you. If the press were to –

IRIS. No, of course. I'll speak to him.

IRIS *battles her rage and nausea.* HELEN *starts combing her hair.*

HELEN. War's made a lot of people change their minds on things. Don't take it too badly. It isn't personal.

IRIS. No, of course.

HELEN *tuts, tosses her comb down, the teeth have snapped.*

HELEN. Another one broken. I do think we could do better on combs, that's my third this month. Come on.

She propels a shell-shocked IRIS *out into the foyer.*

I'll telephone you in the morning, will you be at home?

IRIS. No, I have my clinic.

HELEN. All right, I'll try you there.

GRAHAM HAWES MP (*sixties*) *is waiting with a newspaper,* HELEN *waves to him.* GLADYS *comes forward with* HELEN's *briefcase. She takes it, kisses* IRIS *and crosses to meet* GRAHAM. *They smile at each other, as they exit together.*

GLADYS *leans into* IRIS, *whispers:*

ACT ONE 19

GLADYS. He buys her clothes for her, you know.

IRIS *gives her a look, won't have Helen gossiped about.*

IRIS. Well we know who to blame then, don't we?

Two

The refreshment room at Paddington Station. IRIS *picks up the public telephone, waits for the operator, as, in the background, an* OFFICE GIRL *approaches a man at a table. He is* GEORGE BLYTHE *(fifty-three). The* OFFICE GIRL *says a few shy words to him. He looks up, smiles, signs the paper she holds out. She rushes off, giddy.*

IRIS. Bridgnorth six-two-seven-nine.

GEORGE *goes back to his newspaper.* IRIS *does not notice, as her call is connected.*

Hello, Julian? It's me.

Split stage to JULIAN ELCOCK, *at home in the Elcocks' house.* JULIAN *(fifty-two) has a badly mangled foot and walks with a stick. There is also a metal plate in his head.*

JULIAN. Hi, darling. Go all right? By the way, Shirley rang about the Whitsun holiday. Filey's out but Blackpool might work.

IRIS. Lovely – darling, Helen told me something extraordinary, she said you'd gone over to the 'No's.

Pause.

She showed me a letter you've been sending out, do you...?

Pause.

JULIAN. Yes, I've been meaning to speak to you about that.

IRIS. Meaning to – when?

JULIAN. This line's awful, where are you?

Irritated, IRIS *yanks at the phone cord. Behind her,* GEORGE *is leaving the refreshment room. He says something to the* OFFICE GIRL *on the way out and she screams with laughter.*

IRIS. Only this is the first I've heard of it, and the plebiscite is weeks away, so when exactly where you planning on telling me?

JULIAN. Well you see, this is it, I knew / you'd react hysterically –

IRIS. You do understand what this looks like for me? Sorry, 'hysterically'? I've been working on the Health bill for *three years* –

JULIAN. Well, I was a doctor for years before I even met you, / Iris, so –

IRIS. Yes, and what does that / have to –

JULIAN. It means the last time I checked, being married to you didn't forbid me from having my own opinions.

A whistle, offstage.

IRIS. My train's leaving. I'll see you at home.

JULIAN. Iris –

IRIS *hangs up, marches to the counter.*

IRIS. Whiskey, please.

WAITRESS. We've only brandy.

IRIS. That's fine.

The WAITRESS *pours it,* IRIS *slides some coins to her, and drinks it off in one. A holler offstage,* IRIS *runs – in her haste she stumbles, turns her ankle, cries out.*

WAITRESS. Are you all right, miss? Here, sit down –

IRIS. Thank you, I'm all right. I'm all right. I'm quite all right.

Offstage, the whistle blows again. IRIS *limps out painfully.*

Three

Train compartment. Night. Bitter cold. IRIS *hobbles in, in pain.* GEORGE *is the only other occupant, head tipped back, eyes closed. A Greek newspaper on his lap.* IRIS *sits as far away as possible from him.*

She eases off her shoe, rubs her ankle. Stretches her leg out and rests her foot on the seat opposite. Examines her tender ankle with a grimace.

She leans back and takes in GEORGE, *asleep. He has a face anyone would want to gaze at, and this is what* IRIS *does. He is beautifully dressed. His whole being is an elegant cape over a great clumsy sadness.*

He suddenly opens his eyes. IRIS *is embarrassed to be caught staring, she looks away, coughs. She retracts her leg, embarrassed, eases her shoe on.*

GEORGE. Excuse me, do you know if this is a stopping service?

He has an absolutely beautiful voice. Like yards of blue velvet. An Englishman who has grown more English in exile.

IRIS. Um, yes I believe it is.

GEORGE. If I freeze to death, throw me off at Bridgnorth, won't you?

IRIS. Excuse me?

GEORGE. If I freeze to death, throw me off at Bridgnorth.

IRIS. Oh. Yes, that's my stop too.

GEORGE. Even better. You can drag me home to Mother.

IRIS *laughs, uncertain. He stares at her injured leg.*

You've a ladder in your stocking.

IRIS. Yes, I turned my ankle.

GEORGE. Bad luck. Keep it elevated. Or something.

He closes his eyes and seems to sleep again. IRIS *takes off her shoe again and puts her foot back on the seat, takes out her book and pretends to read, while stealing glances at him. The train jolts along.*

Four

Elcock kitchen. The middle of the night. IRIS *stirs a pan of milk. Pours it into a cup.* JULIAN *enters in dressing gown, slippers and pyjamas. Watches her warily. She avoids his eyes.*

IRIS. I'm sorry, did I wake you?

JULIAN. I couldn't sleep anyway.

A deafening, passive-aggressive silence. He gets a bottle of whiskey, a tumbler. Sits. Pours a drink. Watches her tip a measure of Veronal into the milk.

You're limping.

IRIS. Turned my ankle.

IRIS *rubs arnica on her ankle.* JULIAN *watches.*

JULIAN. That was a rotten way for you to find out, I'm sorry.

IRIS. I'm sorry too. Only to hear it from Helen like that, it was so shaming, Julian –

JULIAN. Yes. I am sorry. Honestly.

IRIS *forces herself to radiate calm. She pours whiskey into her milk.*

IRIS. Darling. Please don't. There are so many doctors against us already.

JULIAN *sighs and shifts, uncomfortable. A long pause.*

When did this, um. When did you change your mind?

JULIAN. After the election I suppose. I realised it might actually go through. What that meant for me.

IRIS. But, but you'll be compensated. We both will. We won't suffer for it –

JULIAN. Excuse me, I am suffering, I'm being forced to become an employee of the state, some bunch of weasel apparatchiks telling me I can never hope to earn more than three hundred pounds, for the rest of my life, however hard I work, however dedicated I am, all because Mr Bevan believes that's the only way to serve the greater good. Well I'm sorry, but I've a metal plate in my head for the greater good. I've a ruined foot for the greater / bloody good –

IRIS. I know, darling, / but –

JULIAN. I know you think he walks on water, but these are the facts: he's mishandling this badly, Iris, he's alienating half the doctors in the country, he needs us and he won't get us, / not like this –

IRIS. Those aren't facts, they're opinions, they aren't even *your* opinions, / so –

JULIAN (*a laugh, disbelief*). They are my opinions. They are / absolutely my –

IRIS. They didn't used to be your / opinions, is all I'm –

JULIAN. I knew it, I knew you'd do this.

IRIS. Do what?

JULIAN. That tone.

IRIS. What tone?

JULIAN. There's just a tone you have sometimes and / it just –

IRIS. What tone?

JULIAN. The tone, that tone you have which suggests you're the oracle at Delphi and I'm a bloody halfwit!

Pause.

IRIS. I thought we believed in the same things –

JULIAN. Don't be so emotional.

IRIS. But it is emotional. It's people dying, in pain, suffering for years because they can't afford a doctor, women miscarrying, bleeding to death because there's no money for the hospital, parents living in agony so there'll always be sixpence for the children –

JULIAN. I know that, but it's a bad Act, Iris! Oh bloody hell –

Suddenly JULIAN *is gripped with pain from his foot, he swallows a howl.*

IRIS. Let me call Ronnie.

JULIAN. No.

IRIS. A different consultant then.

JULIAN. Not having another op.

IRIS. What about medication?

JULIAN. Pills.

IRIS. Yes, pills.

JULIAN. No thank you.

IRIS. So we simply tolerate this, do we?

JULIAN. Tolerate me?

IRIS. I didn't say you, I said this –

JULIAN. I'm so sorry, I didn't realise I was intolerable, how awful for you.

IRIS. Not for me, actually, for you – if it's not your foot, it's the headaches, every bit of you in pain and you won't *do* anything about it!

JULIAN. It's just this dreadful weather. The cold makes it worse.

IRIS. I'm not just talking about the pains, there are, there have been changes. / Perhaps this is part of that –

JULIAN. You know there's a lot *I* tolerate. There's quite a lot other husbands wouldn't put up with / that I –

IRIS. What do you put up with? What do you tolerate? Honestly, I'd like to know. Is your house too clean? Are your meals too hot?

JULIAN *throws his glass against the wall.*

JULIAN. JESUS CHRIST, I TOLERATE YOUR FUCKING AMBITION DON'T I! YOU CAN TOLERATE MINE!

Pause. The ceiling creaks above them, the sound of footsteps.

IRIS. It's all right, darling! Just Mummy being clumsy! Back to bed.

Pause. JULIAN *reaches for* IRIS*'s hand. Smiles.* IRIS *is thrown by his friendliness.*

JULIAN. Oh by the way, the woman from over the fence came round. Mrs, um –

IRIS. Thwaite? The divorced woman?

JULIAN. Yes. She wants us to cut down the cherry tree.

IRIS. It's a hundred years old. Whatever for?

JULIAN. The way it leans. It's right over the fence. Blocks out the light from her onion patch. I went out and looked at it, she's right.

IRIS. Do we have to?

JULIAN. Depends whether you want to make an enemy of her, I suppose.

IRIS. Well of course not. I feel rather sorry for her. She always looks so pathetic, but that tree is –

JULIAN *suddenly cries out in pain. He flexes his leg and covers his eyes.* IRIS *kneels beside him.*

It's all right, darling. It's all right.

Expertly, IRIS *massages his foot. The pain eases. She watches him, anxious. He opens his eyes. She's helped. He breathes, in relief. Manages a weak smile.*

JULIAN. Stupid isn't it? I still can't bear to even look at the thing. Not much of a medical man, am I?

LAURA *creeps in, in her nightdress.*

You should be in bed, Lanky.

LAURA. I can't sleep.

IRIS. It's all right. (*To* JULIAN.) You go up.

> JULIAN *stands, with difficulty.* IRIS *hands him his stick. He goes out.* IRIS *pours the rest of the milk from the pan into another cup, gives it to* LAURA. *They sit together.* LAURA *sips her milk.* IRIS *rubs her eyes.*

LAURA. Did you go to London today, Mummy?

IRIS. Yes, darling.

Pause.

LAURA. Are you going next Wednesday?

IRIS. Yes, after my clinic.

Pause.

LAURA. Did you know, um, Princess Elizabeth's w-wedding dress is on display in London?

IRIS. Yes, I believe you've mentioned it one or two hundred times.

LAURA. I just thought you would want to know.

IRIS. I couldn't be less interested, but that's sweet of you, darling.

Pause.

LAURA. It's at St James's Palace. In a glass case.

IRIS. Is it.

LAURA. The train is thirteen feet long.

IRIS. Come on, drink up, please.

LAURA. Um, are you, will you go to see it?

IRIS. I shouldn't think so, Mummy is very busy working on her London days.

Pause.

LAURA. You know, *I'd* like to see it.

IRIS. I know you would. Drink up. Back to bed please.

She takes LAURA's *cup as* LAURA *goes out. The phone rings,* IRIS *picks it up.*

Doctor Elcock speaking.

Split stage to JUDY STOPES, *Iris's secretary, in nightwear and rollers.*

JUDY. Doctor Elcock, it's Judy, I'm sorry it's so late.

IRIS. That's all right, what is it, house call?

JUDY. Yes, Doctor Mannion telephoned, it's one of his patients, elderly lady, her son found her on the floor, but she's insisting she'll only see a woman doctor, will you take it?

IRIS. Yes, of course. What is it, gynaecological?

JUDY. Doctor Mannion says she won't say but she kept saying it isn't urgent. Do you have a pencil?

IRIS *rummages for a pencil in her handbag.*

IRIS. Old women always say it isn't urgent. Walking round wearing a nappy, 'oh, no, it isn't urgent'.

She finds her pencil.

All right, go ahead.

Five

Howells house. Night. MRS HOWELLS, *a woman in her seventies with a long grey plait, ushers* IRIS *in.* MRS HOWELLS *has a bad cut to her forehead. She has a Shropshire accent and walks with what can only be described as a waddle.*

IRIS. Good evening, Mrs Howells, I'm Doctor Elcock, how are you?

MRS HOWELLS. I told him not to trouble the doctor. Only a few scrapes.

IRIS. Yes, that one on your head looks nasty.

IRIS *takes out a torch.* MRS HOWELLS *drinks from what looks like a glass of water.*

MRS HOWELLS. Oh, that's nothing.

IRIS. Best to make sure, tricky things, head injuries, do you mind?

As IRIS *shines the torch in her eyes, examines her pupils:*

Do you have a headache?

MRS HOWELLS. No.

IRIS. Neck ache?

MRS HOWELLS. No.

IRIS. Have you experienced any nausea or vomiting?

MRS HOWELLS. No.

IRIS (*re: glass*). No, let me take that for you, do you feel drowsy or lethargic?

IRIS *takes the glass from* MRS HOWELLS *as she takes her pulse. She gives the glass a surreptitious sniff.*

MRS HOWELLS. No.

IRIS. Any slurring of the speech?

MRS HOWELLS *gives a disdainful tut.*

Not feeling confused / or –

MRS HOWELLS *whips her wrist away.*

MRS HOWELLS. No. I told you, just a silly accident. I'm sorry to waste your time.

IRIS. Not at all. I only wondered why you especially wanted a woman doctor, Mrs Howells.

MRS HOWELLS. I didn't ring you up. It was my son. He can afford to throw money away, I suppose. You're the Labour woman, aren't you? I didn't vote for you. No thank you. Disgusting, how this country's treated Mr Churchill.

IRIS. He's a fine man.

ACT ONE   29

MRS HOWELLS. He is. I wept when your lot got in. Honestly, I wept. And here we are, bread on the ration, potatoes.

IRIS. How are things with your private functions, Mrs Howells?

MRS HOWELLS. Middle of the war, we never had potatoes on the ration. If that's Socialism, I don't want it.

IRIS. Some ladies of your age, they / find that –

MRS HOWELLS. Yes but you can't be running to the doctor for every little thing, can you? Bankrupt yourself.

IRIS. Well quite. But as I'm here. Might be worth a brief examination. What do you say? I shall be very quick.

Pause. Then MRS HOWELLS *nods. Takes another gulp of 'water'.*

IRIS *takes a bar of soap from her bag and washes her hands. She lays a sheet over the settee and invites* MRS HOWELLS *to lie down.*

Please.

She examines MRS HOWELLS. *As she does so:*

Are you getting out much, Mrs Howells?

MRS HOWELLS. As much as I can. Your hands are cold as death.

IRIS. I'm sorry. Bad circulation. Good pastry, all done now, you can sit up.

MRS HOWELLS *sits up, as* GEORGE *enters in rolled-up shirtsleeves, covered in coal dust, carrying a full coal scuttle.*

GEORGE. Oh.

IRIS *recognises him from the train, it throws her a little. A flicker of confusion for him too, but he can't place her.*

IRIS. How do you do, I'm Doctor Elcock, uh – Doctor Mannion telephoned me.

GEORGE. Yes, thank you – I wasn't expecting you to come till the morning, I was just – uh –

He puts down the coal scuttle, takes out a beautiful pink silk handkerchief, wipes his hands on it. A pause, he is still trying to place her.

(*To* MRS HOWELLS.) Are you being cooperative, Queenie?

MRS HOWELLS. Naturally.

GEORGE (*to* IRIS). I think she's had a fall, but –

IRIS. May I have a word, Mr...?

GEORGE. Blythe. George Blythe.

MRS HOWELLS. I want my bed. (*To* GEORGE.) Be careful. She's a Socialist.

MRS HOWELLS *exits*. GEORGE *smiles, rolls down his sleeves.*

GEORGE. Are you really? How thrilling. Tell me, do you cook the babies before you eat them? I must say it's marvellous of you to come so quickly. Do you. Is / she –

IRIS. Your mother needs a small operation, that's all.

GEORGE. What is it, her womb or something?

,

IRIS. Uh. Yes. She seems anxious about costs, are you able to –

GEORGE. Yes, of course. But I don't want you to think – I send her money every month, I don't know what she does with it.

IRIS. I suspect she might give some of it to the Conservative Party. Also, she drinks. Gin, I believe, may I wash my hands?

She goes to the sink.

GEORGE. You must think me a very bad son, letting her get into this state.

IRIS. You don't live locally?

She dries her hands. GEORGE *gives her a funny look.*

GEORGE. No, I... uh, my work takes me overseas.

IRIS. Oh, whereabouts?

GEORGE. America. Los Angeles. I'm only visiting. I wasn't expecting…

IRIS. No, of course. And how long are you –

GEORGE. A month that's the, that was the intention. I've been away a long time you know. Working and.
,
We write, weekly, her letters never led me to believe there was anything… nothing at all…

He drifts off, troubled. IRIS *suddenly notices the bottom of her slip showing slightly, she straightens her skirt to cover it.*

IRIS. I'll phone as soon as I've spoken to the consultant.

GEORGE. Thank you.

They shake hands. The touch of his hand makes her bold –

IRIS. What do you work as?

GEORGE. Well, I suppose I'm an actor.

IRIS. Really? In the theatre?

GEORGE. No. In the, well, in the pictures.

IRIS *laughs, embarrassed at her ignorance.*

IRIS. I'm sorry. I almost never get to the cinema.

GEORGE. And I'm almost never ill. It's impossible our paths should've crossed at all. Can I see you home?

IRIS. No, I've got my bicycle.

GEORGE. Can you ride with no hands?

IRIS *laughs.*

IRIS. No, but I've always wanted to. Can you?

GEORGE. I used to be able to.

MRS HOWELLS (*offstage*). George? George? Has she gone?

GEORGE *and* IRIS *stifle a laugh.* GEORGE *whispers:*

GEORGE. You have to go very fast and not be afraid of crashing. That's the secret.

Six

Iris's surgery. A week later. MRS ARBUTHNOT, *a middle-class patient (fifties), lays on the table, staring at the ceiling, detached from her body. She holds her handbag on her stomach even though* IRIS *is giving her a gynaecological exam. A long pause.*

MRS ARBUTHNOT. Were you aware you have a crack?

IRIS. Beg your pardon, Mrs Arbuthnot?

MRS ARBUTHNOT. In your ceiling. There's the most enormous crack.

IRIS. Oh. Yes. This clinic is on the brink of collapse I'm afraid.

MRS ARBUTHNOT *makes an involuntary sound of discomfort.*

I'm sorry. I'm almost finished.

MRS ARBUTHNOT. Is everything all right?

IRIS. Mm-hm.

,

It should be condemned, really.

MRS ARBUTHNOT *raises her torso in alarm.*

The clinic, I mean.

MRS ARBUTHNOT. Oh.

,

IRIS. All right. Well done, you can sit up.

MRS ARBUTHNOT *sits up, tidies herself.*

Tell me, do you enjoy having connection with your husband?

MRS ARBUTHNOT. Why? What is there to enjoy?

Pause. Then IRIS *smiles brightly and writes some notes.*

IRIS. I'm going to prescribe you paracetamol for the pain, and something called progesterone which may do something to help your symptoms.

MRS ARBUTHNOT. Is it safe?

IRIS. Both are perfectly safe.

MRS ARBUTHNOT. Only my maternal grandmother turned blue on paracetamol.

IRIS. It stopped her breathing?

MRS ARBUTHNOT. No. She just turned blue. Head to toe.

IRIS. Well… if that happens… stop taking it.

MRS ARBUTHNOT. Thank you, doctor.

She takes the script and goes. JUDY *sticks her head in, in coat and hat.*

JUDY. Just letting you know I'm here now, Doctor Elcock.

IRIS. Thank you. How did it go?

JUDY. Oh it was dreadful. The drill shakes the floor. I'm saving up to have them all out.

IRIS. Any messages?

JUDY *hands her a sheaf of correspondence.* IRIS *quickly signs the letters.*

JUDY. There's these to sign, and Helen rang, she wants to schedule some cottage meetings before the BMA meeting next week. Oh, and Doctor Mannion phoned, he says your house call with the prolapsed womb was discharged this morning.

IRIS. Mrs Howells? How is she?

JUDY. He said she made the anaesthetist cry but is doing very well.

IRIS *smiles and hands back the signed letters. As* JUDY *turns to leave –*

IRIS. Judy, do we have any magazines in the waiting room?

JUDY. Uh, yes. I mean –

IRIS. Film ones I mean.

JUDY. *Picturegoer*, that sort of thing? Heaps.

IRIS. Would you bring me some?

JUDY. Of course, Doctor Elcock.

She goes out. IRIS *wilts in fatigue for a moment. Then sits up as* JUDY *returns with a stack of* Picturegoer *magazines.*

Those are ever so old, Doctor Elcock, I can get you a new one / if you –

IRIS. Those will do. Did you get the Ribena?

JUDY. Uh... yes, and the bread.

She takes them out of her handbag and puts them on the desk.

IRIS. You're a wonder, thank you.

IRIS *waits for* JUDY *to leave, then quickly riffles through a* Picturegoer. *Nothing in the first one. Nothing in the second, until she finds him on the back page.*

GEORGE *enters, in white tie. He smiles, holds up a bottle of Blatz beer with a smile.*

GEORGE. I've been to Milwaukee many times. And I'm well acquainted with its fine art collection, and fine premium beers. And of *all* of them, my favourite is Blatz. It's Milwaukee's favourite beer. Because it's Milwaukee's finest beer. So enjoy that wonderful, wonderful, wonderful Blatz beer flavour. Today.

GEORGE *goes.* IRIS *flicks through the next magazine. An* AMERICAN REPORTER *enters.*

REPORTER. All the stars came out to the Fox Carthay Circle movie theatre last night for Universa International's premiere of *The Egg and I*, based on the bestselling novel. Leading man Fred MacMurray was joined by Tyrone Power and a whole galaxy of other leading lights.

GEORGE *enters with* SYLVIA SAMUELS (*American, ravishing, late thirties, a siren in evening gown and fur*). *He is holding a giant prop egg.*

Here's Hollywood husband and wife George Blythe and Sylvia Samuels. Sylvia, you've a new picture of your own about to open, *Dance of the Seven Veils,* with Charles Laughton, isn't that right?

SYLVIA. Yes it opens Tuesday night, at the Rivoli.

REPORTER. Now whenever I've met Charles Laughton he pretends to be very gruff, very serious, but is he a warm man?

SYLVIA. Oh, he is.

The REPORTER *pokes* SYLVIA *flirtatiously.*

REPORTER. Now well is it true that this one got him doing a jitterbug? / Is that true?

SYLVIA. Oh! Well no, he got *me* doing it!

REPORTER. Tell me, would you do the Dance of the Seven Veils for us now? Just a little?

SYLVIA *laughs, coy.*

SYLVIA. Oh well I'd love to but I left my veils at home you know.

REPORTER. Okay, well I saw the picture the other night, and I think it's the greatest thing you've ever done, and –

SYLVIA. Thank you very / much.

REPORTER. No I really do think it's terrific, you're terrific, tell me how d'you stop that snake from slithering where you don't want him to slither?

SYLVIA. Well, I have to tell you, that was a very naughty snake.

REPORTER. I'll bet he was.

SYLVIA. No, it was a she.

REPORTER. A girl snake. Fancy that. And I understand you're about to take your first trip to uh, Paris?

SYLVIA. Oh yes. And I can't wait. It's always been very glamorous to me and I've always loved the French language.

REPORTER. Do you speak it?

SYLVIA. Oh, not at all. George does though.

She turns and looks at GEORGE *lovingly. The* REPORTER *remembers* GEORGE *is there.*

GEORGE. Je fais de mon mieux mais je ne parle pas couramment, pas de tout.

,

REPORTER. Uh-huh, I was about to remark that you probably have a whale of a job, keeping up with Sylvia, I notice she's got a sort of tremendous energy, she just burns off the screen, doesn't she?

GEORGE. Oh, she's radiant. Completely radiant. She reminds me of Florence Lawrence, you know, one those marvellous silent movie stars who didn't have to do anything so vulgar as *talk* to tell us a story.

REPORTER. Right, and –

GEORGE. Only of course she does talk.

REPORTER. Uh-huh.

GEORGE. Which is even better.

REPORTER. You're a very lucky man.

GEORGE. I know.

IRIS shuts the magazine. GEORGE *and* SYLVIA *exit.* IRIS *hesitates. Then picks up the phone. Suddenly hangs up again. Pause. Then she picks it up again.*

IRIS. Bridgnorth two-two-one-four.

She waits. The call is connected.

Shirley? It's Iris, how are you, dear?

…

Yes, we're looking forward to it – in fact I wondered if I might ask the most enormous favour?

…

Well, I made a call in your neck of the woods last week to a Mrs Howells, on Norfolk Street? Oh don't you? She's ever

ACT ONE 37

such a sweet old thing, only she seems rather isolated and sort of, you know, cooped up. I wondered, if it wasn't too much of an imposition, if you might invite her too –

…

Oh bless you, yes, she's in the book – oh by the way, one thing, she has her son staying, I believe, visiting from America.

…

Um… George, I think, George Blythe, does that – ?

…

Oh goodness, Shirley, yes I think he is an actor, I'd never heard of him, but –

…

Oh for – you and your crushes!

…

Yes, I suppose you can, and I'll make a fuss over poor old Duncan so he doesn't feel jealous.

…

All right, bye, dear. What's that?

…

Oh, my lilac crêpe. With the buttons down the back.

…

Yes.

…

Yes.

…

Yes I know but I got most of it out and I can just stand with my back to the wall, can't I?

…

All right, dear. Yes. Goodbye.

IRIS *hangs up. She is still for a few moments. Her buzzer sounds.*

JUDY (*offstage*). Mr Rennie for you, Doctor Elcock.

IRIS *quickly scoops the magazines into a drawer.*

IRIS. Yes, send him in.

Seven

Sieves house. The racking sound of croup. IRIS *has just finished examining a baby.* MR SIEVES (*thirty-five going on ninety*) *works a pair of bellows on a fire that is failing to take.*

IRIS. She seems a little better, but let's keep an eye on that croup.

She passes the baby to BARBARA (*twelve*).

Thank you, Barbara. You're a good little mother.

BARBARA. Am I? I don't really like babies.

IRIS. Would you mind taking her outside while I talk to your father?

BARBARA *looks at her father.*

MR SIEVES. Do what she says.

BARBARA *exits with the baby.*

IRIS. Any word from your wife?

MR SIEVES *laughs, humourless, gives up on the bellows, rolls a cigarette. Offstage, the baby starts to cry. The sound grows and grows.*

Have you – would you like me to speak with the police?

MR SIEVES. Why? I've done nothing wrong.

IRIS. No, I wasn't suggesting – only she's been missing for two weeks now, / and –

ACT ONE 39

MR SIEVES. Thirteen days.

IRIS. Even so.

MR SIEVES. And she's not missing, she's AWOL.

IRIS. She could be hurt, / or –

MR SIEVES. She's fine. I had a letter.

IRIS. Did it say when she would be coming back?

MR SIEVES. She's not coming back, is she – Barbara, get back in here!

BARBARA returns with the baby, now screaming. MR SIEVES *takes the baby from her and bounces it on his shoulder grimly.*

Shhh. Shhh. Shhh. Shhh.

Pause.

IRIS. Mr Sieves, I wanted to make you aware of the home-help service, it's free of charge, I'd be happy to arrange it for you.

While MR SIEVES*'s back is turned, she surreptitiously takes the bread and Ribena from her bag. Puts them on the table.* BARBARA*'s face lights up.*

MR SIEVES. We can manage on our own.

IRIS. Of course.

MR SIEVES. I know what you want with all that, you want to control people. Permits for this, permits for that. I had enough of that in the army.

IRIS. Of course.

MR SIEVES. Another thing, I paid out four-and-ten for that bag of coal and half of it's rubbish.

IRIS. Would you like me to –

MR SIEVES. I don't want you to do anything! I don't want you here at all, I'm just saying.

Pause. MR SIEVES *hums 'Daisy Bell (Bicycle Built for Two)' quietly to soothe the baby.*

IRIS. I'm sorry. I'll leave you alone now. Goodbye, Barbara.

IRIS turns to leave.

MR SIEVES. You forgot your things.

IRIS and MR SIEVES look at each other. He keeps humming to the baby. She puts the bread and Ribena back in her basket and goes.

Eight

Ryan house. Night. A small middle-class party in full swing. JULIAN and ERICA, a young middle-class widow, both drinking. 'Open the Door, Richard!' plays on the radiogram.

ERICA. Apricots.

JULIAN. Mmm-hmm.

ERICA. Olives.

JULIAN. Oh yes.

ERICA. Lemons.

JULIAN. Go on.

ERICA. Almonds.

JULIAN. Keep going.

ERICA. Garlic.

JULIAN. Don't stop.

ERICA. Butter.

SHIRLEY RYAN (Julian's sister, fifties) enters with the sherry bottle, topping up.

JULIAN. No! No! She's gone too far! Shirley, this woman, whoever she is, is spreading pornography through your party!

SHIRLEY. It's Erica, you know it's Erica. Top-up, dear?

ERICA *nods,* SHIRLEY *tops up her glass.*

JULIAN. It can't be Erica, Erica is lady captain of the golf club, whereas this harlot has been whispering a stream of absolute filth into my innocent doctor's ears.

SHIRLEY. Is this true, Erica? Are you corrupting my baby brother?

ERICA. Well, I've been *trying* to, only he will keep mentioning his wife.

IRIS *enters in her lilac crêpe dress, bearing a tray of burnt savories.*

SHIRLEY. Oh, bad form.

IRIS. Are my ears burning?

ERICA. Something is.

IRIS. Yes, I'm sorry, the tops have caught a little.

JULIAN. Let me do that, sis.

JULIAN *reaches for the sherry bottle.* SHIRLEY *affectionately slaps his hand away.*

SHIRLEY. Nonsense, you've been on your feet all day, go and sit down and Iris will bring you a plate.

JULIAN. Yes, boss.

JULIAN *exits as* IRIS *hands the tray around. We see the iron burn on her dress.*

ERICA. Still, such a wonderful spread.

SHIRLEY. Well, if I never devil another egg again, it'll be too soon.

ERICA. I do envy you your chickens.

GEORGE *enters, stands watching* IRIS *across the room.*

SHIRLEY. Oh, they're a menace. We only got them because we saw that picture – Duncan, what was it called?

DUNCAN (*offstage*). What?

SHIRLEY. The picture we saw. Claudette Colbert wrestles a pig?

DUNCAN *enters.*

DUNCAN. *The Egg and I.* (*To* GEORGE *as he enters.*) * Have you seen it?

GEORGE. No.

SHIRLEY. *The Egg and I*, thank you, I wish I'd never laid eyes on it, Mr Blythe! How wonderful of you to – you're taller than you look in the – but I imagine that's just a, may I take your coat? Thank you – Pat! Let me get you a coaster!

SHIRLEY *takes* GEORGE's *coat and rushes off.* ERICA *and* DUNCAN *fall into conversation.* GEORGE *approaches, touches* IRIS's *elbow, she turns.*

GEORGE. I suspect this is your doing.

IRIS. Oh, I'm so pleased you could come.

GEORGE. It's very kind of you, it cheered Mum up a lot to be invited.

IRIS. Oh, not at all, where is she?

A pretend horror falls across GEORGE's *features.*

GEORGE. Dammit, I knew I'd forgotten something...

MRS HOWELLS (*offstage*). Mr Churchill should be sitting on the throne of heaven if you ask me... disgusting, the way this country's treated him...

IRIS *laughs.* GEORGE *smiles.*

GEORGE. Drink?

IRIS. Uh, a gimlet, thank you.

IRIS *sits, he makes her a gimlet, one for himself.*

GEORGE. Would you mind if we sat down?

IRIS. Not at all.

GEORGE. Thank you.

They sit.

Cheers.

IRIS. Cheers.

They drink.

GEORGE. The other day… I felt I recognised you, but I can't think how. Have we met before?

IRIS. I don't believe so. But I'm a local councillor, people / often –

GEORGE. Are you?

IRIS. Yes.

GEORGE. God. And a doctor?

IRIS. Yes.

GEORGE *offers her a cigarette, she takes one, he takes one himself, lights them both.*

GEORGE. There are some people put on this earth to make the rest of us feel lazy, aren't there? I expect you throw pots or teach English to refugees in your spare time, do you?

IRIS. No, I'm too busy knitting for orphans.

GEORGE. Ugh. You disgust me.

He smiles, smokes.

That's not it though.

Pause. IRIS *looks at* JULIAN *across the room. Hesitates.*

IRIS. I think maybe… last Wednesday, I was on the London train, I think perhaps you were too.

It suddenly falls into place for GEORGE. *He smiles, amused.*

GEORGE. Oh! Is that it?

IRIS. You caught me gawping at you.

GEORGE (*gallant*). No, I don't think so –

IRIS. Oh, but I was. Shamelessly. I thought, what a nice face that man has, if I wasn't an old married lady I should wake him up and have a good flirt.

They laugh.

GEORGE. You are married then?

IRIS. Oh, terribly married, yes. That's my husband there, Julian.

IRIS *gestures to* JULIAN, GEORGE *surveys him, his stick.*

GEORGE. Army?

IRIS. Navy. Ship's doctor.

GEORGE. Ship got hit, did it?

IRIS. Yes, a torpedo. Kola Peninsula, day before the war ended, Julian was rather lucky to – where did you serve?

GEORGE. Uh, well, I didn't. I'd been in America for some time before it all kicked off and. Well.

Pause.

IRIS. I see. And you never –

GEORGE. No.

,

No.

,

It gets rather tiresome doesn't it?

IRIS. What does?

GEORGE. Everyone going on as if the war were a sacred thing, and anyone who fought in it a saint.

GEORGE *downs his drink.* IRIS *speaks straightforwardly. Simply relating a fact.*

IRIS. Yes, I suppose it must seem rather unattractive from the outside. But I'm afraid when you've spent six years united in a cause you all believe in, people who haven't don't seem quite real. The English, you know. They love a reason to disapprove. I shouldn't take it to heart. Why didn't you serve?

ACT ONE 45

GEORGE *laughs, surprised.*

I'm sorry, was that –

GEORGE. No, it's just – every person I've met since I came back has tied themselves in knots avoiding that question. It's a relief to have someone just come out with it.

IRIS. Well?

GEORGE. What?

IRIS. Why didn't you serve?

Pause.

GEORGE. Because I am a shit.

Pause. He produces a smile. 'Where or When' by Peggy Lee starts playing on the radiogram.

Do you go to London every week?

IRIS. Every Wednesday, yes.

GEORGE. Are you going tomorrow?

IRIS. Um, I think – yes. Why?

GEORGE. Well, it just so happens I am as well. I have an audition at two o'clock at the Gainsborough Studios – it's dreck, but it's a thousand pounds for twelve weeks.

IRIS. Goodness. What's the film?

GEORGE. Oh. *Bluebeard's Honeymoon.* Women's picture. Melodrama. Did you see *Mrs Gibson's Ghost*?

IRIS. No.

GEORGE. Oh. Well it's like that but less realistic.

IRIS. Makes you proud though, doesn't it?

GEORGE. What does?

IRIS. That we can make pictures here as well as Hollywood.

GEORGE. I shouldn't think anyone is going to be particularly proud of *Bluebeard's Honeymoon.* Not that you will see it.

IRIS. I did see one, a few years ago, the lovely man with the sad eyes and the woman who wears hats so well?

She looks at GEORGE, *but he shakes his head, he can't guess.*

She had two very irritating children and there was a lot of business in a train station?

GEORGE. *Brief Encounter*?

IRIS. That's it. I did think that was marvellous.

GEORGE. Really?

IRIS. Oh, I sobbed. Didn't you?

GEORGE. It seemed unrealistic to me.

IRIS. The chemistry between them was wonderful, I thought.

GEORGE. Well exactly. In real life they wouldn't have made it to the third act without fucking.

Pause. IRIS *looks at him. Not shocked, but amused.*

IRIS. If they'd done that, it wouldn't have been a tragedy.

Pause. Then they both laugh, embarrassed.

GEORGE. I'm so sorry, this is my fourth drink.

IRIS. I'd better catch up.

GEORGE. And I feel as if I've known you for years. Isn't that odd?

IRIS. Very. Aren't you going back to America?

GEORGE. I don't want to leave Mum until she's better.

IRIS. That's good of you.

GEORGE. Yes, well. She brought me into the great wide world. Can't owe a person much more than that. (*Sotto.*) Also, I'm winning an absolute fortune off her at whist.

IRIS *smiles. A hesitation.*

IRIS. Won't your wife miss you?

GEORGE *tenses. He looks up.* JULIAN *is approaching.* IRIS *glances round, sees.*

I'm afraid I'm very busy on my London days. Good luck with your audition.

GEORGE *squeezes her bare upper arm, stands up.*

GEORGE. Thank you. (*To* JULIAN.) Excuse me, I must get my mother to release our host from her jaws.

GEORGE *moves off.* JULIAN *sits beside* IRIS. *She holds the place on her arm that* GEORGE *squeezed.*

JULIAN. You look done in. Helen works you too hard. Spinster ladies don't understand the demands of a family, you should stand up to her more.

IRIS. Yes, I expect you're right.

Pause. IRIS *covertly watches* GEORGE *across the room.*

JULIAN. Shirley says we're on for Blackpool in May, by the way. She's found a lady with rooms for all of us, breakfast and hot water included.

IRIS. Lovely.

Pause. They have nothing to say to each other. SHIRLEY *comes bustling over.*

SHIRLEY (*sotto*). I can't believe it. I keep looking at him standing by my Aunt Dolly's china elephant and thinking: that's George Blythe, standing by my Aunt Dolly's china elephant.

JULIAN. Time for a top-up, I think.

JULIAN *lurches off.*

SHIRLEY. He's older than he looks on screen but still. Very attractive. Imagine funny little Mrs Howells having a son like that. I saw you holding him rapt, I'm green with envy, what did he say to you?

IRIS. Oh. Nothing much. About his mother, you know, and… the war…

DUNCAN *approaches.*

DUNCAN. Iris, I wonder if you could take a quick squiz at something for me?

IRIS. Your back?

DUNCAN. Yes. It's got rather larger since I saw you last.

IRIS moves DUNCAN into a more private spot, and examines his back.

SHIRLEY. Nothing about the wife?

IRIS. No. Why? (*To* DUNCAN.) Does it hurt when I do that?

She touches the growth. He shakes his head.

SHIRLEY. She's not made a picture for more than a year. Disappeared, gone into retirement or something.

IRIS. Having a baby probably. Doesn't want anyone to see her getting fat. Is it itchy?

DUNCAN. A little.

SHIRLEY. No, I heard in the hairdresser, they're in the middle of a divorce.

DUNCAN. You'll be in the middle of one too if you don't shut up.

SHIRLEY pats him.

SHIRLEY. Promises, promises!

DUNCAN (*to* IRIS). What do you think?

IRIS. Nothing to worry about. But I'd like to freeze it off. Could you come to the surgery next week?

DUNCAN. Of course. Thank you.

SHIRLEY. Can't you wait six months? Then we might get it done for free.

SHIRLEY slips her arm through IRIS*'s, a conspiratorial whisper:*

What does he smell like?

Pause.

IRIS. Sweat.

Nine

Helen's office, House of Commons. Wednesday. IRIS *reads aloud to* HELEN:

IRIS. '…Many people sympathise with the sick person. Everyone wants the poverty-stricken mother to find a house for her children. But too many of us have assumed the resolution of these difficulties was entirely the responsibility of the individual concerned. But if we transform all these private headaches into public ones… then we can get something done.'

She looks up at HELEN.

HELEN. Yes. Fine.

IRIS. But?

HELEN. You sound like a suicidal head girl.

IRIS *slumps in an armchair, lights a cigarette.*

IRIS. We can't all have your talents. I can't even convince my own husband on the Health Service.

She picks up a newspaper from the arm of the chair, reads aloud:

'The Doctors Say "No". Not so much a landslide as an avalanche.'

She tosses the paper down, despondent.

HELEN. It's going to happen.

IRIS. It's ridiculous, they can't even decide whether the entire Act is an unspeakable affront or if the Act is good except for four or five minor details!

HELEN. Nye says he'll stuff their mouths with gold if he has to.

IRIS *laughs.*

IRIS. He will as well, won't he?

HELEN. Expect so.

Pause.

IRIS. Helen, you've been so kind to me –

HELEN. Don't be disgusting. I'm never kind to anyone.

IRIS. But don't you think you've put your money on the wrong horse?

HELEN. You're no worse at the oratory than Clem. Did you hear him on the radio last night? I switched over to the boxing halfway through.

IRIS. It's not just that. I get to the end of every day and feel I've done a hundred things poorly rather than one thing well.

HELEN. So give up the doctoring.

IRIS. I can't.

HELEN. Why not?

IRIS. Because that's the bit I'm good at.

HELEN. Well then work harder at the other. And do it quickly, because they asked me not to tell you, but Ivan's thinking of stepping down.

IRIS. Seriously?

HELEN. There, that's put a ferret in your knickers hasn't it.

IRIS. What have you heard?

HELEN. His kidneys. His wife wants to take him to the Netherlands for some sort of treatment.

IRIS. And do you think – would they – is it even possible I could –

HELEN. Be selected? Certainly, if you learn to speak in full sentences.

IRIS paces, rapidly calculating, trying to curb her excitement.

IRIS. We only just hung on to that seat in forty-five. The majority is tiny. They wouldn't risk a woman, an unproved woman, would they?

HELEN. I'm hearing otherwise.

IRIS. But what about Hector?

HELEN. Hector's liked, of course. But they want a choice of candidate.

IRIS. Have they said – what have they said?

HELEN. You didn't hear it from me. But I think you have a crack at it. Family woman, local doctor.

IRIS. Lot of Catholics round there.

HELEN. So?

IRIS. So I've probably given out more cervical caps than they've said Hail Marys.

HELEN. I expect half the Hail Marys were said in prayer for cervical caps.

IRIS. Oh, Helen…

HELEN. Well, it's not definite yet, but it's looking pretty likely. William is going to move the writ within the next six months. You'd better speak to Julian. Get your ducks in a row.

IRIS. Yes. Of course.

,

HELEN. He's a good stick. He'll get behind you, I'm sure.

IRIS. Yes I'm sure.

,

HELEN. By the way, I met a woman, your neighbour, Mrs Thwaite. Rather worked up about a tree, I said I'd speak to you.

IRIS. Oh, I'm sorry you were bothered with that.

HELEN. I don't mind. Interesting woman. She was very funny about the Mothers' Union.

IRIS. Why?

HELEN. Oh, they've kicked her out. Silly bitches. I've asked her to come and char for me twice a week.

IRIS. Really?

HELEN. She's divorced, Iris, not contagious.

IRIS. No, I only meant – doesn't her husband give her any money?

HELEN. He gives her enough for the children. She wants to save for a holiday, I was telling her about the Via Alpina.

IRIS disappears into her own head for a few moments.

Penny for them?

IRIS. What? Oh, nothing, I was just. Hoping Julian remembered I left some soup for his lunch.

HELEN. Damn, is it one o'clock already?

IRIS looks at her watch.

IRIS. Actually, Helen, would you mind if I slipped away early? Only Laura had a temperature when I left this morning, Mrs Creevey's there but –

The phone starts to ring, HELEN *gestures to* IRIS *– 'Go, go' – answers the phone with a cockney accent.*

HELEN. Miss Mackeson's office, Beryl speaking, how may I help you?

IRIS gathers her coat and hat hurriedly. HELEN *resumes her own accent, laughs.*

Yes, it is me, however did you guess?

IRIS rushes out.

Ten

Outside the Gainsborough Studios. Bitter cold. Through the railings we can see various pieces of equipment, rails of costumes, cameras being moved between sound stages. IRIS *has been waiting some time.* GEORGE *finally comes out. He sees her with surprise.*

GEORGE. Hello.

IRIS *is embarrassed, self-conscious. A fake laugh.*

IRIS. Oh, I wondered if I'd see you! I had a meeting nearby and I thought – I've never seen a film studio before. It's very exciting, all the…

She gestures, vaguely.

How did it go?

GEORGE. Oh. Awful. Awful. They offered me the part.

IRIS *notices he is carrying a Greek newspaper under his arm.*

IRIS. Do you speak Greek?

GEORGE. Hm? Oh, no, that's just my disguise. Anyone who recognises me, they take a closer look and realise it isn't me at all, it's just some Greek chap who looks like me. Works rather well.

IRIS. But you don't even look Greek.

GEORGE. No, I know, peculiar isn't it? Shall we walk? It's bitter.

They start to walk.

IRIS. I'm an odd bird, I don't feel the cold much.

GEORGE. Like a puffin.

A DUSTMAN *wheels a dustcart through, stops to sweep the ground.*

IRIS. Do you get recognised a lot?

GEORGE. Not so much here. It's worse when I have a picture out.

IRIS. Do you have one out now?

GEORGE. Yes, but it's only a very small role, blink / and you –

IRIS. Oh look!

She fishes a discarded banana skin out of the dustcart, waves it joyfully.

I haven't seen one of these since before the war!

GEORGE *smiles.* IRIS *discovers the* DUSTMAN *looking at her. She tosses the banana skin back into the cart, wipes her hands. The* DUSTMAN *exits.*

GEORGE. Have you finished your work for the day?

IRIS. Yes.

She suddenly clutches her stomach, embarrassed.

I'm so sorry.

GEORGE. What for?

IRIS. My stomach rumbled, didn't you hear it?

GEORGE. I thought a Messerschmitt was going over. Hungry?

IRIS. No, not really.

GEORGE. You were brought up like me. Lower-middle-class politeness. If you wanted something very much you always said you didn't.

,

But a body does need feeding, you know.

They look at each other.

Eleven

Fleming's Restaurant, Oxford Street. The wallpaper hangs off in strips. The white linen on the table is stained and mended. GEORGE *and* IRIS *at a table.* IRIS *picks gloomily at an anaemic portion of fish gratin.*

IRIS. I'm sorry. It used to be a treat to eat here.

GEORGE. What are you talking about? This is wonderful. Look at how grey my soup is!

She laughs, he reaches for his cigarettes. IRIS *catches sight of the beautiful pink silk lining of his jacket. A flash of luxury.* IRIS *puts down her knife and fork.*

What's the matter?

IRIS. I suddenly feel embarrassed.

GEORGE. What on earth of?

IRIS. Of… us. What we must look like. Our clothes are worn, our food tastes of nothing, and I felt you looking at me and I suddenly felt ashamed. And then I felt angry for feeling like that because really we haven't anything to be ashamed of.

GEORGE. Austerity's all right during a war. Much harder to swallow in peacetime.

IRIS. Well exactly.

GEORGE. I blame the politicians.

IRIS. So do the public, I'm afraid.

GEORGE. Surely not.

IRIS. No, they hate us. All the Labour Party is to most people is shortages and queues.

GEORGE. And hope, surely? They voted for you, after all.

IRIS. Hope for what?

GEORGE. Whatever you're peddling, I suppose.

IRIS. Oh, you mean a fair and equal society?

GEORGE. Is that all?

IRIS laughs, hollow. Folds her napkin carefully.

IRIS. Do you know what I think? This country will never be equal, because the people with the most to gain can't stomach what it will take to win it, not really. Not if it means a period of discomfort, or broken combs, or too much fat in a tin of sausage meat, it's too much, after what they've been through already. Meanwhile the whole country goes about worshipping a royal family kept in luxury while children go hungry and the price of coal rises.

GEORGE. That's a rather bleak diagnosis.

IRIS. It is bleak. We're losing. It's terribly hard to have a revolution, do you have a cigarette?

GEORGE gives her a cigarette, leans across the table and lights it.

I'm sorry. I'm being… something.

GEORGE. Yes. You are, but I like it.

She rests her hand on the table. He lays his hand in front of it so the very tip of his finger touches the very tip of hers. IRIS stares at the table.

They stay like that for some time.

A WAITER approaches. IRIS moves her hand. GEORGE lights a cigarette.

Has it occurred to you that you have a problem of storytelling, not politics?

IRIS. That isn't really my forte, I'm afraid.

GEORGE. Isn't it? Mr Churchill, for example. Mother worships him, personally I think he's a warmonger and a snob, but you can't deny he's a first-class storyteller.

IRIS. He certainly has memorised a lot of Tennyson.

GEORGE. Oh come on! He flung a Union Jack over a hamster and made us all think it was a lion. He did a page-one rewrite on the English character and convinced you all you weren't a nation of dull shopkeepers, but righteous heroes with fire in your hearts and iron in your bowels, and didn't you all lap it up?

IRIS. Yes, well, I personally think Nye is the superior orator.

GEORGE. Yes, he is, he's very good. He's the best you've got, but he isn't prime minister is he? Attlee is. The other team have got Orson Welles in the lead while you've got Charlie Ruggles.

IRIS. Who?

GEORGE. Exactly.

IRIS. We must have told a fairly good story in 1945 or we wouldn't be in power today.

GEORGE. Mathematics has never been my strong suit. But that's three years ago and elections happen every four. The first thing you learn in Hollywood is that if the public like something, you have to keep churning out more of it.

IRIS. I sometimes think if Nye were leader of the party / then –

GEORGE. Then he still wouldn't be as popular as Churchill. The English will always be in thrall to the upper classes.

IRIS. How depressing.

GEORGE. Yes but it'll never change so you may as well get on with it.

IRIS. I shall have to. My daughter has developed a mania for Princess Elizabeth and her wretched dress.

GEORGE *laughs. So does* IRIS.

GEORGE. What's her name?

IRIS. Laura.

GEORGE. What's she like?

IRIS. Oh, sweet. Stubborn. A bit silly. She's pretty but she's not curious.

GEORGE. I'm sorry.

IRIS. It's my fault. I'm not an especially good mother, I don't think.

GEORGE. Well. You're a wonderful role model for her.

IRIS *laughs at the idea. Downs her drink.*

IRIS. She'll probably be all right, she'll marry at eighteen, some nice, bland man, and get through the rest of her life like any other average girl, doping herself at the pictures three times a week.

GEORGE. Oh, thank you.

IRIS. What? Isn't that the point of pictures? To give young women with dull lives something to think about while they sit on production lines or stand over the washing-up bowl?

GEORGE. Not at all. They go to the pictures to feel the rapture of being alive. That's why I go, anyway. When rapture is hard to come by elsewhere, that is.

IRIS. Well… there you are, I'm only asking, if they have to depend on fantasy to tolerate real life, shouldn't we be trying to make real life a little better? To make it happy, and not merely tolerable?

He smiles. She wipes her mouth on her napkin, self-conscious.

Do you have a vote in America?

GEORGE *makes a face – 'Who knows?'*

Don't you believe in anything?

GEORGE. If you mean Tories, Labour, that sort of thing, no I don't. I follow it, but I don't care for it, I find it boring, frankly, but I do know you can't scold grown men and women into eating broccoli when ice cream is available.

IRIS. Am I the broccoli?

GEORGE. Yes I'm afraid you are, gorgeous. You promise righteousness but no pleasure. You are green and unknown and overboiled.

ACT ONE 59

IRIS. Terribly good for you.

GEORGE. Oh, fuck good for you. 'Good for you' is the Left's problem. When people are poor, tired, struggling, they're naturally Conservative. It's not political, it's biological. A human body seeks a warm, familiar place over a cold, strange one.

IRIS. Even if the warm familiar place is a house on fire and the cold strange one is a palace?

GEORGE. A cold palace. A cold half-built palace. Only architects can look at blueprints and see majesty, the rest of us just see terrifying squiggles.

IRIS. So how does one conjure the palace before it's been built?

GEORGE. Like I say. Tell them a story. Tell them a story in which they can imagine themselves happy, not virtuous. Tell them a story in which they are lit beautifully and make-up have done wonders with their double chin and all the gowns are by Adrian and if you must go on about sausage meat, make it aspirational sausage meat. Make it glamorous. Make it thrilling. I don't know, just bloody *move* people.

IRIS. I think that's exactly what we did in 1945.

GEORGE. Oh for Christ's – 1945, / 1945 –

IRIS. And in case you weren't aware, we are about to deliver a healthcare system to beat anything in the world.

GEORGE. All very sexy. And in a year's time, when the country wakes up from its VE Day hangover, and remembers its place, and starts tugging its forelock again, they'll kick you out of bed and not even give you the cab fare home.

IRIS. So what would you say?

GEORGE. I wouldn't say anything, the whole thing bores me to tears.

IRIS. I can't tell if you're being facetious for the sake of it or if you really mean it.

GEORGE. Both.

IRIS. You don't live in this country. You didn't fight our war. Your work is very interesting, and while I'm sure you could play a certain type of politician very well –

GEORGE (*delighted*). Greasy, no doubt?

IRIS. – I think you have rather a superficial grasp of the issues facing real ones.

GEORGE. All right, have it your way, do we want coffee?

IRIS. No thank you.

Pause. A shift in GEORGE's *body.*

GEORGE. 'Greed has poisoned men's souls, has barricaded the world with hate, has goose-stepped us into misery and bloodshed. We have developed speed, but we have shut ourselves in. Machinery that gives abundance has left us in want. Our knowledge has made us cynical. Our cleverness, hard and unkind. We think too much and feel too little. More than machinery we need humanity. More than cleverness we need kindness and gentleness. Without these qualities, life will be violent and all will be lost.

Don't give yourselves to brutes – men who despise you – enslave you – who regiment your lives – tell you what to do – what to think and what to feel! Who drill you – diet you – treat you like cattle, use you as cannon fodder. Don't give yourselves to these unnatural men – machine men with machine minds and machine hearts! You are not machines! You are men! You have the love of humanity in your hearts! You don't hate! Only the unloved hate – the unloved and the unnatural! Don't fight for slavery! Fight for liberty!'

Pause. IRIS *is entranced, in spite of herself.*

IRIS. That was very… was that Michael Foot?

GEORGE. Charlie Chaplin. You really do need to go to the cinema more often.

He drains his soup. IRIS *laughs, embarrassed. The air is cleared.*

IRIS. What's the name of your picture? The one out now, I mean?

GEORGE. *Acapulco Lady*. But it really isn't 'my' picture, except for about two minutes in the middle.

IRIS. Do you have to get home to your mother?

GEORGE. No, I'm fifty-three.

She gives him a withering look.

She isn't expecting me. Why?

IRIS *smiles. Puts her hand up to signal for the bill.*

Twelve

A cinema. IRIS *drags* GEORGE *to his seat, the newsreel already playing.*

GEORGE. Iris, please, this is humiliating.

IRIS. Oh, come on! I want to see if you're any good.

GEORGE. Well I'm not, so now you know, let's go and get a drink or something –

IRIS. Anyway I thought you only had a small part. You can close your eyes for that bit.

GEORGE. I don't see my pictures, I never see my pictures.

IRIS. Whyever not?

GEORGE. Because the idea of looking at my own face for that length of time makes me want to vomit.

IRIS. Nonsense. Don't you want to feel the rapture of being alive?

GEORGE. I can assure you, *Acapulco Lady* is devoid of rapture.

IRIS. Shhh.

They watch. He is sulking. She keeps looking at him, trying to thaw him. Then the newsreel ends and –

The Pathé film from the Prologue begins to run. IRIS'*s face falls in mortification as she sees her own face writ vast on the screen.* GEORGE *is overcome with laughter.*

She stands up, tries to leave, he pulls her down again.

Please. Please, I can't –

GEORGE. No, you made your bed, you can lie in it.

IRIS *watches through her fingers. All in whispers:*

IRIS. Look at my teeth, my awful teeth.

GEORGE. I've got jackets on mine, see? The studio paid for them.

He bares his perfect white gnashers at her.

IRIS. How do you bear it? Bad enough looking at one's face in the mirror, let alone blown up to ten feet tall. Ugh I can't watch.

She turns her face away so she is looking at GEORGE.

GEORGE. I told you, I don't see my pictures, I only act in them.

IRIS *watches his face as his eyes remain fixed on the screen.*

IRIS. Please, stop looking.

GEORGE. Why? I'm enjoying the view.

IRIS (*voice, on screen*) '…And of course the other thing is, you must have a very cooperative husband! (*Laughter.*) But I've got one of those so I'm very lucky…'

GEORGE. Your husband sounds like a saint. If you were my wife I would keep you barefoot and pregnant.

IRIS. I shall be forty-nine next birthday, biology is against you.

GEORGE. Barefoot and deliciously fat then.

IRIS. You're against working women?

GEORGE. I was talking about you in particular, it isn't a general position.

An USHER *casts a torch beam over them and shushes them.* GEORGE *ironically copies the shush at* IRIS. *Looks back at the screen.* IRIS *examines his profile. Lowers her voice –*

IRIS. Your wife works.

GEORGE. Yes, but she was an actress, at least she did something useful.

IRIS. And medicine and politics aren't useful occupations?

GEORGE. I would allow the medicine but not the politics. It's why I like Hollywood, Hollywood is an apolitical town. Does it bring joy, does it bring pleasure, does it bring escape from the general dreariness of life? That's all anyone cares about there.

IRIS. Does it make money, surely?

GEORGE. Nothing wrong with money.

IRIS. That's the Conservative manifesto, I thought you weren't political. You said 'did'.

GEORGE. What?

IRIS. You said your wife did something useful, has she given it up?

GEORGE. She has rather a lot on her plate at present.

IRIS. Is she having a baby?

GEORGE....

IRIS. Are you divorcing her?

GEORGE. It's rather complicated.

IRIS. Do you love her?

Pause. The feature starts. An orchestral score in the background.

GEORGE. I'll always love her in some way, I expect. Do you love your husband?

Pause.

IRIS. Yes, of course.

A long pause. Then:

GEORGE. You weren't bad on camera you know. Put Vaseline on your teeth next time. Makes them whiter.

Thirteen

Train compartment. IRIS *and* GEORGE *take their seats on the train home. Evening.*

IRIS. Do you always play men like that?

GEORGE. Rotters, you mean? No, sometimes I play cads too. And bounders, I'm terribly good at bounders. Apparently I am very credible as a moral vacuum.

IRIS *laughs.*

IRIS. Poor soul. Do you miss America?

GEORGE. Very much. If it wasn't for Mum, I don't think I'd ever come back to England again.

IRIS. You don't sound as if you grew up in Shropshire.

GEORGE. Hm. RADA rather kicked it out of me.

Pause. GEORGE *suddenly stands up. In his native Shropshire accent:*

'Oh, when I was in love with you,
   Then I was clean and brave,
And miles around the wonder grew
   How well did I behave.

And now the fancy passes by,
   And nothing will remain,
And miles around they'll say that I
   Am quite myself again.'

IRIS *looks at him. He sits down. A long pause.*

A. E. Housman.

IRIS. I know.

GEORGE. Dreary bugger.

Pause. They look at each other. A blossoming. The possibility of a kiss. Then the moment is cauterised.

IRIS. I'm sorry, I'm going to be very rude, I've ever such a lot of reading to do.

GEORGE. Not at all, it's important I get to grips with Bluebeard's motivations. I expect they're very complex.

He takes out a script, she takes out her papers, they settle to their work. GEORGE *lights a cigarette. He offers her his case, she takes one. He lights it for her.*

The conductor, REYNOLDS *(forties), enters the compartment.*

REYNOLDS. Tickets, please.

They hold out their tickets, he punches them. As he hands them back.

It's Doctor Elcock, isn't it?

IRIS *looks up, jolted. She can't place him, smiles.*

Reynolds. I came to see you about the railings outside the bowls club, you won't remember / me but –

IRIS. Mr Reynolds, of course I remember you, how lovely to see you, I believe the issue was resolved in the end, was it?

REYNOLDS. Yes, I've been meaning to write to thank you, only I've not been well.

IRIS. I am sorry. Nothing serious I hope?

REYNOLDS. Oh, no, just… my old trouble. I won't go into it.
,

It's gastric, that's all I'll say, and – anyway, I saw you get on, I thought I would take the opportunity –

He looks at GEORGE.

– beg pardon, I'm interrupting you and your… the gentleman here.

IRIS. Excuse me, this is my cousin, Mr –

GEORGE (*Greek accent*). Kyrgios. Pleasure to meeting you.

REYNOLDS *glances at* GEORGE*'s Greek newspaper.*

IRIS. Nick is visiting for a few weeks, he's giving a talk at Birmingham, he's a university lecturer.

REYNOLDS. Oh, in what?

IRIS (*immediately*). Pre-modern religious iconography.

REYNOLDS *looks at* GEORGE. GEORGE *beams back a smile.*

GEORGE. I like very much Birmingham!

REYNOLDS. Yes. You must make sure you see the Leather Museum.

GEORGE. Yes, you spell for me please?

GEORGE *thrusts the newspaper and a pencil at him. As* REYNOLDS *writes in the margin,* GEORGE *and* IRIS *steal a look at each other, suppressing wild laughter.*

REYNOLDS. There you are.

He hands the newspaper back to GEORGE. GEORGE *squints at his writing. Pause.*

Well I'll say goodnight.

IRIS. Good evening.

GEORGE. Thank you for the pleasures. Goodbye for ever.

REYNOLDS *exits.* IRIS *and* GEORGE *laugh.*

You are a frighteningly good liar.

IRIS. I would say the same to you.

She looks down, realises her pen has leaked blue ink over her fingers.

Dammit, this blasted pen –

GEORGE *takes out a silk handkerchief.*

GEORGE. Let me.

IRIS. No don't! Your beautiful handkerchief –

But GEORGE *takes her hands, does his best to wipe them clean. She watches him.*

REYNOLDS (*offstage*). Shrewsbury. All change for Shrewsbury.

IRIS *suddenly kisses* GEORGE. *An embrace.* IRIS *breaks it.*

IRIS. I'm sorry. I – I'm so sorry.

Suddenly panicked, she exits. GEORGE *sits there. Folds up his handkerchief.*

GEORGE. Scheiße.

Fourteen

Iris's surgery. The next day. IRIS *is stuffing envelopes, tuts as she gives herself a paper cut, sucks it. Her eyes fall on a pot of Vaseline on her desk. She goes to the mirror. Smears Vaseline over her teeth. Smiles at her reflection. The phone rings, she quickly scrubs her teeth, picks it up.*

IRIS. Doctor Elcock speaking.

Stage splits to reveal GEORGE *in a public telephone box.*

GEORGE. It's me.

,

IRIS. Hullo. I'm sorry about last night.

GEORGE. Next Wednesday, are you going to London again?

IRIS. Yes, I expect so.

GEORGE. Do you have plans for the evening?

IRIS. The sessions tend to run late, so –

GEORGE. Could you bunk off? I have to see an old friend in a play, I think it might be your sort of thing. Lots of heartfelt speeches and mahogany furniture.

Pause.

IRIS. How kind, my sister-in-law loves the theatre, perhaps we could all –

GEORGE. I'm afraid I only have two tickets.

IRIS. Oh that's a shame.

GEORGE. Yes, isn't it.

Pause. IRIS *sucks at her paper cut.*

Fifteen

A West End theatre. JEAN (*thirties*) *is giving an overwrought performance in a contemporary play.*

JEAN. 'Tell us we're gloomy, tell us we're glum. Say our food is bland, our clothes shabby – grey people beneath a grey sky. But for crying out loud can't you see we're trying to do something extraordinary – to have a revolution without a guillotine!'

A round of applause.

Dressing room. After the performance, GEORGE *and* IRIS *wait for* JEAN.

GEORGE. What did you think?

IRIS. Rather earnest.

GEORGE. Yes, that's why I thought it would be up your street.

IRIS. Why?

GEORGE. Because you're rather earnest.

IRIS. God, I don't sound like that, do I?

GEORGE. No comment.

IRIS. What about you? Did you like the play?

GEORGE. Oh, God no. Terrible, turgid –

JEAN enters. GEORGE leaps to his feet.

Wonderful! Wonderful! You did it again!

GEORGE embraces JEAN. IRIS hovers, a little awkwardly. JEAN is voluptuous, easy-mannered, energetic. She bustles about in her silken robe, pouring champagne.

JEAN. You hated it, didn't you? (*To* IRIS.) He loathes the theatre, I don't know why he bothers coming. By the way I love that hat, it's darling.

GEORGE. Jean, Iris, Iris, Jean.

JEAN. Well at least you remember my name today!

They share a laugh at an in-joke as JEAN hands IRIS a glass of champagne. IRIS touches her hat, self-conscious.

How's dear Sylvia? I haven't had a peep from her for months and months. I do hope you haven't knocked her up, it'll ruin her career.

GEORGE. No, I've just been beating her senseless, I've locked her in a bedroom till the bruises subside.

JEAN, pleasantly scandalised, looks at IRIS wide-eyed.

JEAN. You awful man!

IRIS. Indeed. I thought the play was very interesting.

JEAN's robe threatens to gape, she fixes it, unselfconscious.

JEAN. Yes, I'm rather fond of it in a way. It's my first time playing a really intellectual sort of woman. (*To* GEORGE.) It's like you with the Nazis, I usually only get the airheads.

IRIS. Have you played many Nazis?

GEORGE. Oh, heaps. I am the go-to man for bullet-headed Prussians. Nobody, it seems, can enunciate the word 'Schweinehund' quite as feelingly as I.

JEAN *laughs. Puts an arm around* GEORGE, *kisses his head amicably.*

JEAN. Poor darling. At least there's more variety in villains than in always being the blonde with a bosom.

GEORGE. My dear, you always appear to find infinite variety within your bosom. And don't forget, sometimes you play redheads.

JEAN *hits him playfully and squeals with laughter.*

JEAN. Oh, he's dreadful, isn't he?!

IRIS *smiles, forced.*

IRIS. Yes isn't he.

Sixteen

Bus stop. Night. IRIS *and* GEORGE *sit, waiting. A long, charged silence. He offers her a cigarette. She shakes her head without looking at him.*

GEORGE. Is something the matter?

IRIS. Not at all.

GEORGE. Jean's nothing but a kid sister to me, if that's what you're –

IRIS. What a shame. I'd have thought she was exactly your type –

GEORGE. Oh, I didn't know / I had a type.

IRIS. – beautiful and trivial and laughing like a drain at anything a man says, however inane, however offensive.

GEORGE. Yes, that does sound appealing doesn't it?

IRIS. I don't know why you don't go back there, she clearly adores you, I shouldn't think you'd have to beg.

ACT ONE 71

GEORGE. Yes, but unfortunately I tend to fall in love with sour-tempered middle-aged married women as a rule.

IRIS looks at him. Shaken. She looks away, fumbles in her handbag.

IRIS. What a silly thing to say.

GEORGE. I'm sorry. It rather slipped out.

Her hands shake. GEORGE *takes out his cigarette case, takes one out for her. Lights it for her, hands it over, she smokes.*

Iris.

He reaches for her, she pulls away –

IRIS. Let's not make a song and dance of it, it was a slip of the tongue.

GEORGE. Yes, I'm sorry. But I do mean it. I have, I mean. Fallen in love with you. I think. I thought you already knew but –

IRIS. Please, this is humiliating.

GEORGE. Why?

IRIS. Because you're having a joke, at / my expense –

GEORGE. That's not –

IRIS. And I'm sure it's very funny but it's rather / cruel and –

GEORGE. It isn't a joke. I don't mean to / humiliate you –

IRIS. Don't.

GEORGE. But –

IRIS. Please *don't*.

IRIS turns away, covers her face, trying not to cry.

GEORGE. I'm sorry. I was selfish, asking you to come tonight. But you were so brave, coming to the studio that day. It made me brave too. Darling Iris.

Pause.

I'm not free to leave my wife. I don't think I ever will be.

IRIS. Yes, of course. I'm not free either, / so –

GEORGE. Aren't you?

IRIS. No.

,

No, I – you're still in love with her then?

GEORGE. No. I'm not sure I ever have been, not like this. But she's always been very decent to me, and I can't cast her aside when the only thing she's done wrong is not being you.

They look at each other. He walks towards her. She freezes, unable to move. He strokes some strands of hair away from her face. He kisses her. She kisses him back.

IRIS. Why couldn't you?

GEORGE. What?

IRIS. Why couldn't you leave her? She's young, / she's successful, beautiful –

GEORGE. Because I could never look myself in the face again. And you couldn't look at me either.

IRIS. You can't know that, / you can't possibly know that.

GEORGE. Maybe not at first. Maybe it would take months, but soon enough any grain of desire, any wretched scrap of me that was attractive or interesting or worthy of you would dissolve, and one day you'd see nothing but a shabby old bounder without an ounce of basic human decency.

IRIS. I'm not some sort of Victorian. I'm not a prude, people get divorced, people leave / their wives –

GEORGE. Not like this. / Not like this.

IRIS. She would forgive you. I would forgive you.

GEORGE. WELL I FUCKING WOULDN'T.

Pause. GEORGE *regrets his explosion.*

Iris, / I'm sorry –

IRIS. I love you.

Of course I love you.

Please never call me again.

She runs out. He watches her go.

Interval.

ACT TWO

One

Blackpool Beach. Three months later. Whitsun. 15th May 1948.

IRIS, JULIAN, SHIRLEY *and* LAURA *in deckchairs on the sand, in the sun.* LAURA *reads the newspaper aloud.*

LAURA. 'The National Health Service is saved. That is the upshot of the doctors' second pleb– pleb– p–'

IRIS. Plebiscite.

JULIAN. Let her get it.

LAURA. 'Plebiscite. The service has still many ob-sta-cles before it; but at least it should be able to make a prompt start on July fifth. A manjority' – when is Uncle Duncan coming back with the ices?

IRIS. I don't know, carry on please.

LAURA. 'A manjority of the professhon are still against the… terms of service. But the adverse manjority has… diminshed so markedly since the February vote that the B-M-A Council has decided to advise the doctors to co– co– co– co– co–'

IRIS (*quickly*) 'Cooperate', that's enough, darling, well done, see if Aunt Shirley wants a cup of tea, will you?

LAURA. Would you like a cup of tea, Aunt Shirley?

SHIRLEY. I won't say no.

JULIAN *takes the newspaper back as* LAURA *unpacks a Thermos.*

You look done in, Iris.

IRIS. Oh dear, do I? Too much sun, maybe.

LAURA *gives* SHIRLEY *a cup of tea.*

SHIRLEY. Thank you, dear.

LAURA. Can I go and look at the donkeys, Mummy?

IRIS. Yes but don't come back sobbing again, they're not sad, their eyes just look like that.

LAURA exits. Uncomfortable, IRIS takes off her jacket. Her armpits are wet with sweat. SHIRLEY watches a holidaymaker in the distance.

SHIRLEY. Goodness swimsuits are small this year. *She's* not on the ration, is she? Do you have a match?

IRIS gives her some matches, she lights a cigarette.

Do you know, I was waiting with the luggage at the train station, I asked a porter for a light, he lit my cigarette, then winked at me and asked if I wanted to hear him imitate a pheasant.

IRIS. What?

SHIRLEY. I said no thank you.

IRIS. And what did he say?

SHIRLEY. He did it anyway, I have to say it was uncanny. People are so romantic about the working classes since the war but when you actually meet one, they often seem rather bovine. And yet apparently the whole country must be reordered around them.

JULIAN (*sotto*). And she's off...

SHIRLEY. Meanwhile it's to hell with the middle classes. To hell with their way of life, their pleasures, I mean Blackpool's fine I suppose, but before the war we went to France you know, every year, it was heaven.

IRIS. Was it?

SHIRLEY. Oh, heaven! But there you are, we've given up our car, our library subscriptions, Duncan's given up his golf, we haven't any sort of home help at all you know, poor Duncan gets bubble and squeak three times a week.

JULIAN. It's a war on the middle class.

SHIRLEY. I know you're ribbing me but that is my feeling, yes. All this grandiose talk, but what have you really done?

IRIS. We've built eight hundred and eighty thousand houses.

JULIAN (*sotto*). With other people's money.

IRIS. We've introduced pensions, sickness benefit, funeral benefits, unemployment / benefits –

JULIAN (*louder*). The people's money.

IRIS. Taxes, yes –

JULIAN. Taxes, exactly, the government didn't pay for them, we paid for them. The Labour Party didn't earn that money, it's not their bloody *largesse.*

IRIS. I'm sure Shirley doesn't need to hear us quarrelling, darling!

SHIRLEY. Oh, I knew the pendulum would swing back. It was only when he met you he became a Bolshevik, you know.

JULIAN. Don't talk rubbish, sis.

SHIRLEY. It isn't rubbish. Muv thought it was ever so romantic you know, she wrote to me, she said Julie is looking so handsome at the moment, he has fallen head over heels for a Socialist and now he drinks beer straight out of the bottle.

JULIAN. If you weren't a Socialist after the Depression you were a bloody savage. The economy was on fire.

SHIRLEY. Well, call me a savage then, but it's a good job you sold your practice before they got hold of the country or you'd be stuck doing kitchen-table amputations in a mining village with no money.

IRIS. Who wants to / make a sandcastle?

JULIAN. I didn't sell it to make money, I sold it because I'd done what I set out to do.

SHIRLEY. Which was?

JULIAN. You know what it was.

SHIRLEY. Yes but I love hearing you say it.

JULIAN. So you can make fun of it!

SHIRLEY. Of course so I can make fun of it! I'm your older sister, that's what I was put on / this earth to –

IRIS. For God's sake, can't you drop it? He sold it because he'd dragged a ramshackle surgery next to a slag heap into the twentieth century! Because he'd worked himself into the ground for ten years so that the working-class children he saw weren't an inch shorter than the middle-class ones! Because I asked him to, so we could live somewhere that would tolerate a woman doctor, because he was idealistic and pigheaded and wonderful, now can we please shut up about it?

Pause. JULIAN *and* SHIRLEY *exchange a look.*

SHIRLEY. Where *can* Duncan be with those ices?

JULIAN. It's rather a long walk to the kiosk.

SHIRLEY. I wish we hadn't bothered. They'll be all melted down his arms by the time he gets back and what shall we do then?

IRIS. You could lick it off.

SHIRLEY. Beg pardon?

IRIS. You could lick the ice cream off his arms.

Pause.

SHIRLEY. By the way, my friend Mary Secombe was convinced she'd seen you at the theatre, isn't that funny? I told her, Iris doesn't care for culture, mind you this was some fervid left-wing thing, it might have been your cup of tea, whether one can have a revolution without bloodshed, sort of *King Lear* without the lovely gory bits.

JULIAN. You can't.

SHIRLEY. Can't what, darling?

JULIAN. Can't have a revolution without bloodshed. If there's no blood, it's not really a revolution. Oi! Lanky-Legs. Let your old dad lean on you.

SHIRLEY. All right, darling, don't get your shoes wet again.

> LAURA *comes running,* JULIAN *either exits or moves away with her, down to the tideline.* IRIS *and* SHIRLEY *watch* JULIAN *looking out to sea.*

Is he still having the pains?

IRIS. Yes, sometimes.

SHIRLEY. The foot?

IRIS. Mostly his head lately. From the plate, you know.

SHIRLEY. Oh dear, what a bind. And there's nothing they / can –

IRIS. He's had enough of hospitals for the time being, I think.

SHIRLEY. Poor baby. Extraordinary he can bear to even be near water, isn't it? After what he went through.

IRIS. Yes.

SHIRLEY. Sometimes I have dreams about it, isn't that silly? I can see him, frantically paddling, and all around him the sea is on fire and the water is black and full of bodies, but I can't reach him and then the explosion happens and I wake up and I can't bear it. It leaves me sobbing, the idea of not being able to help him.

IRIS. You're his big sister. Natural you want to protect him.

SHIRLEY. Yes. If anyone ever hurt him, I think I would stab them you know. I'd enjoy it.

,

You know you really do look absolutely raddled, dear.

She looks beyond IRIS.

Oh at last! Here comes Duncan.

Two

Helen's cottage. Day. IRIS *calls to* HELEN *in the next room.*

IRIS. Of course now we need fifty thousand nurses we don't have, the ones we *do* have are terrified they're to be flung all over the country, and then there's the consultant shortage problem, we're down in pathology, radiology, anaesthetics, paediatrics –

MRS THWAITE *enters with mop and bucket, in headscarf, rubber gloves, an apron.*

Oh. Hello.

MRS THWAITE. It's Mrs Elcock, isn't it?

As they talk, MRS THWAITE *empties her bucket and slowly transforms. She takes off her headscarf, puts on a chic hat, exchanges her rubber gloves for leather ones, puts on a beautiful red coat in a New Look silhouette.*

IRIS. Yes. You must be Mrs Thwaite.

MRS THWAITE. Your local leper.

IRIS. Oh… no… I –

MRS THWAITE. It's when it's in leaf. That's the issue.

IRIS. Excuse me?

MRS THWAITE. Your tree. It puts the whole garden in shade. I couldn't grow a thing last year. I know it's lovely, but I thought perhaps you could move it or something?

IRIS. It's very old. It wouldn't survive a move, I don't think.

HELEN *enters, bearing a tray of three gin and tonics.*

HELEN. Oh good, you've met. Time for a ginny, don't you think? Can I make one for you, Rachel?

MRS THWAITE. No, thanks. Gin makes me violent. I'll see you next week.

HELEN. All right. Key under the geranium if I'm not back.

MRS THWAITE *exits.* HELEN *gives* IRIS *a gin.*

So you've patched it up with Julian, have you?

IRIS. There's nothing to patch up. One doesn't have to agree with one's husband on everything, does one? Or does one?

HELEN. Good. I was worried. Ivan's out. William's moving the writ.

IRIS. Really? When?

HELEN. This week. This is it. By-election within six weeks. The selection committee is sitting next Friday. I've given them your name. Cheers.

She grins, drinks. IRIS *is overwhelmed. She takes a swig of gin, gathers her things.*

Don't go. I've made parsnip goulash.

IRIS. I have to start preparing. Who's on the committee?

HELEN. It'll be two locals and an up-from-London I expect.

IRIS. I won't let you down.

HELEN. I know you won't.

IRIS *takes a breath, nervous and exhilarated. Off, a cough.*

IRIS. Is Graham here?

HELEN. He's giving a speech in Ludlow in the morning, I'm to drive him over.

IRIS *gives her a look.* HELEN *gives her one back.*

IRIS. Be careful. People notice.

HELEN. Iris, I spend my days with a head full of statistics about dead babies and why Blackpool has twice the rate of diphtheria of West Ham. I must be allowed some fun. Anyway it's only friendship really. Unfortunately I've always had the sort of body with which men find it difficult to remain platonic.

IRIS *looks at her, muffled in her fur coat. The sex and life in her.* GRAHAM *enters.*

GRAHAM. Hullo, Iris. You've caught the sun.

He points to the gin and tonic in HELEN's *hand.*

I hope that's for me?

She gives it to him. They kiss. IRIS *watches them. Then looks away, embarrassed.*

Three

A panel of three senior Labour Party members, MR FLACK, MR JESSUP *and* MR CLEGG, *await* IRIS. *She enters. They rise to shake her hand.*

MR FLACK. Mrs Elcock.

IRIS shakes their hands in turn.

IRIS. Good morning. Good morning. Good morning.

MR FLACK. Please, take a seat.

IRIS takes a seat.

Thank you for coming to talk to us today.

MR CLEGG. We were pleased to see your name on the shortlist.

IRIS. Oh, thank you, excuse me.

She turns away to cough a little.

MR FLACK. You look nervous.

IRIS. Oh, and here I was thinking I was hiding it so well!

MR FLACK *and* MR CLEGG *laugh.*

MR FLACK. Nothing to be nervous about.

IRIS. I've imagined being in front of you all so many times. It's hard to believe it's actually happening.

MR JESSUP *yawns.* IRIS *glances at him.*

MR FLACK. Well then I'll kick off, nice easy one to start with, what campaigning experience do you have?

IRIS. Well, I was Miss Mackeson's campaign manager in forty-five, as you know she won with rather a large majority.

MR CLEGG. Four and a half thousand, something like that, wasn't it?

IRIS. Rather more actually, nearer five. And of course I campaigned myself at a local level as a councillor, which was a wonderful opportunity to meet the community on their own doorsteps.

MR FLACK. And what sort of help did you have?

IRIS. It was really just myself and my husband and a rather overworked mimeograph machine to be honest!

IRIS, MR FLACK and MR CLEGG laugh.

MR FLACK. And your husband, he's happy is he?

IRIS. Well –

MR CLEGG. He'll be at your side, for speaking engagements and so forth, is what Mr Flack means.

MR FLACK. Holding your hand. Cheering you on.

IRIS. Yes. If he's not busy with his own work of course.

,

MR CLEGG. Difficult, I imagine, to keep all the plates spinning?

,

IRIS. Yes. A little.

Pause. The MEN *take notes.*

MR FLACK. Mr Clegg, your question.

MR CLEGG. Thank you, Mr Flack, Mrs Elcock, what made you want to become a Member of Parliament?

IRIS. Well, I don't really.

,

Sorry, what I mean to say is, I'm not particularly drawn to parliamentary life in itself. It's rather inconvenient, with a family, you know, but I can't see any other way to help people in the way I want to.

MR CLEGG. You don't find that satisfaction in your medical work?

IRIS. I used to, yes. But lately… I find myself putting sticking plasters over wounds that needn't have been caused in the first place. Illnesses and impairments that could easily have been prevented by better housing, better food, education, welfare – or diseases of the spirit – just, sort of, broken people, you know, and there's nothing in my bag that can fix that.

MR CLEGG. So you've tired of one profession, and think politics might be more… glamorous perhaps?

IRIS. No, that's not – I'm not expressing myself very – what I mean is just… I don't feel like a doctor. I feel like a housewife with a mop and bucket and burst plumbing and I spend all day, every day, trying to clean up the mess and tape up the pipes, when really, the whole house needs rebuilding.

The MEN *take more notes. For longer this time.*

MR FLACK. Mr Jessup? Do you have any –

But MR JESSUP *shakes his head.*

No. Well I think we've heard enough to –

MR CLEGG *whispers in his ear. He nods.*

Very well, do you mind one last question, Mrs Elcock?

IRIS. Of course.

MR FLACK. What do you think about the New Look?

IRIS. I'm sorry?

MR FLACK. The New Look.

MR CLEGG. Christian Dior.

MR FLACK. What would you say if asked about it?

IRIS. I would wonder whether you asked the gentlemen on the shortlist the same question.

MR FLACK. We did, as it happens.

MR CLEGG. They were, quite frankly, baffled.

MR FLACK. We thought you might have some more illuminating thoughts.

IRIS. I'm not sure I have any thoughts on it at all.

MR FLACK. Take a moment, if you like.

,

IRIS. I spent three days memorising the GDP of every country in Europe for this.

MR CLEGG. We appreciate your rigour.

IRIS. But you want me to hold forth on Parisian fashions, very well, I think it's ridiculous. I think it's a waste of fabric and manpower and designed to make ordinary women feel inadequate, as if ordinary women didn't already spend most of their lives feeling inadequate, British women haven't agitated for the longer skirt, frankly we're glad for any new clothes at all and most women would prefer we put our efforts into more important things.

MR FLACK. Thank you. / That's –

IRIS. I mean it's very beautiful of course. Don't you think?

An uncertain mumble from MR CLEGG *and* MR FLACK. IRIS *cuts into it.*

Yes, yes, but more than anything it reminds me of the Victorians. That long skirt and the tiny waist. People think they like it because it's daring and modern, but actually they like it because it reminds them of their grandmothers. It makes them feel as if they still lived in a comfortable, powerful time, you know, when we were ruling an empire rather than losing one, that sort of thing – it's nostalgic really, nostalgic and romantic and ravishing, of course, but as I said thoroughly Victorian and it is my heartfelt belief that the Victorian era is exactly what we must drag this country out of. Out of workhouses and malnutrition and rickets and baby farms, out

ACT TWO 85

of the deserving poor and the undeserving poor, out of a class system nobody can ever traverse let alone escape, out of war veterans reduced to selling matchboxes on the street, out of polite savagery, out of behaving as if some people just *deserve* to live amongst rats, in rags, in damp, in disease, we have to drag it, kicking and screaming, into a future in which nobody, however they are dressed, is left behind, because what the hell did we go through that war for otherwise? And how *dare* we call ourselves civilised if we don't?

Pause.

MR JESSUP. Hear hear.

Four

A street in Shropshire. BOB DANVERS-WALKER *enters, narrating into a mic.*

BOB. To South Shropshire, the question-mark Midlands constituency, turn the eyes of the nation, for this forty-eighth by-election will measure the trend in Britain's political thought. A battle of no excuses, it's touch and go from the start. The Conservatives, in candidate Anthony Heap, are testing not only Labour's hold on a seat won from the Tories only three years ago, but also their grip on Britain's electorate.

IRIS *appears, waving to her constituents, and shaking the hand of a* GIRL *who runs out with a 'VOTE ELCOCK' banner.* JULIAN *stands behind her, head down.*

With an election less than two years away, on the eve of the launch of the National Health Service, the Socialists, with their candidate, Doctor Iris Elcock, seen here with her husband, are also fighting with an eye to 1950. As both campaigns reach their climax, the Tories play a trump card. A visit by Winston Churchill, with an all-out attack on Socialist overspending.

WINSTON CHURCHILL *enters, speaks into a loudhailer.*

WINSTON. We will be voting for the revival of our name and repute all over the world.

IRIS *speaks into her own loudhailer.*

IRIS. I have the greatest respect for Mr Heap, and Mr Churchill, of course. But both speeches we have heard from them today have very largely been concerned with the notion that life in this country was better in the past. I find this rather a bold claim. But I believe something even bolder. I believe that life might be better in the future. And what they call ignorance, I call hope. What they call overspending, I call investment. Not in the pockets of plutocrats. But in you. Your health. Your homes. Your children. Your dignity.

A wave of applause engulfs her.

Five

Elcock bedroom. Night. A pair of twin beds. IRIS *and* JULIAN *undress in silence.*

JULIAN. Well, we got through that.

They get into bed. He picks up a book and starts reading.

IRIS. Yes. Thank you for being there. It was decent of you.

She gets into bed. Watches him for some time.

JULIAN. Did you want the light out?

IRIS *climbs out of her bed, into his, and kisses him.* JULIAN *puts down his book. She kisses him again, more passionately. He pulls her to him. They kiss.* IRIS *slips her hand under the sheet. She works hard, trying to get something to happen. Eventually –*

It's all right.

IRIS *continues.*

I said all right.

Pause. IRIS *smiles and kisses him.*

IRIS. It doesn't matter.

He pulls her to him, they lie in silence. Eventually, she opens her mouth –

JULIAN. Please don't give me one of your speeches.

IRIS. I wasn't going to. It hasn't even been / that long –

JULIAN. I don't want to discuss it.

IRIS. Darling, please –

JULIAN. No.

IRIS. Couldn't we just talk to someone –

JULIAN. No!

IRIS. We don't even know what the problem / is –

JULIAN. I know what the problem is. I hate your body. It was never your main attraction and now I can't, if you want the truth of it, I can't stand it. I've tried to be kind, but you don't stop, pawing at me all the, is it any surprise I don't want to make love with you? The clothes you walk around in, stains and, and laddered stockings and drab, actually, that's what – I look at you and I just see this drab… thing, and I'm supposed to just spring into action am I? When you click your fingers, I should – groping at me all the – I'll tell you when I want you to touch me, is that too much to ask?

,

I said is that too much to / ask?

IRIS. No.

JULIAN. No. Good.

,

Good.

,

Anyway, people get very hung up on sex life. Lots more important things in a marriage than that.

Pause.

I'm sorry. That came out rather colder than I meant it. But you'd rather I said it, wouldn't you? (*An attempt at teasing.*) I know how you feel about me bottling things up!

IRIS *forces a laugh.*

IRIS. Yes.

Pause.

JULIAN. Do you want to read?

IRIS. No.

JULIAN. Do you mind if I put out the light?

IRIS. No.

JULIAN *turns out the light. Silence. Then, in the dark:*

I meant to say, I met Mrs Thwaite last week. At Helen's.

JULIAN. Oh yes.

IRIS. She was wearing the most beautiful red coat.

Pause.

JULIAN. What about the tree, did she mention it?

IRIS. What? Oh that. Yes. Chop it down.

Six

Sieves house. Day. MRS SIEVES *has returned to the home. Thirties, brittle, eroded. She's watching* LAURA *singing lustily as* MR SIEVES *does up his boots.*

LAURA.
'We are the boys and girls well known as minors of the ABC
And every Saturday all line up
To see the films we like and shout aloud with glee
We like to laugh and have our sing-song
Just a happy crowd are we

We're all pals together.
We're minors of the ABC!'

Pause.

You can get in for free if you sneak in the fire exit. Maybe your children could do that.

IRIS enters with the baby, hands her to MRS SIEVES.

IRIS. She's gaining weight very nicely, well done, and there's no sign of that croup coming back. Where's Barbara today?

MRS SIEVES. She cleans for a woman in High Town, Saturdays.

MR SIEVES. I'm not paying for this. We never asked you to come.

MR SIEVES goes out. IRIS takes an EC1 form from her bag.

IRIS. I just wanted make sure you'd filled out one of these. You don't have to register with me, but you should register with someone. After July the fifth it's free for everyone. Laura, take the baby outside for some fresh air, won't you?

LAURA (*sighs*). Is she very heavy?

IRIS. Do as you're told, please, darling.

LAURA sighs, takes the baby and exits. MRS SIEVES takes the form from IRIS, looks at it for a long time. IRIS watches her. Eventually:

MRS SIEVES. Expect you think my behaviour was shocking.

IRIS. No. When wives feel unable to cope... there's often a reason.

MRS SIEVES. Yes, well. Life's no harder for me than anyone else, but it just. Gets you down. You know? Queueing and queueing and then I was in the tripe queue and I thought when's it going to end? When's it...?

She takes a deep breath.

And I thought 'never', that's when. It just took me very sudden. I went to my old friend Berenice in Congleton. I went to the pictures four times in a week.

IRIS. What did you see?

MRS SIEVES. I don't... I can't even remember now, they all wash over you don't they, is it important?

IRIS *shakes her head.*

My husband doesn't like you coming. He says you're a Socialist.

IRIS. You voted for Mr Churchill, I imagine.

MRS SIEVES. I worship that man.

IRIS. Naturally.

MRS SIEVES. But I voted for your lot.

IRIS. Oh.

MRS SIEVES *picks up the form again.*

MRS SIEVES. Can I come too or is it just for the children?

IRIS. It's for everyone. After the fifth of July, there'll be no charge for anything.

MRS SIEVES. You're sure are you?

IRIS. Yes.

MRS SIEVES. I'm sorry. I just. I had a.

,

I had a little boy, older than Barbara, he, his appendix burst, he was seven, day of the funeral they sent me a bill for the ambulance, no I'm all right.

She blows her nose. Pause.

I miss the war. I miss it so much, isn't that wicked of me? I hate this house. I hate this town, I hate the hills. I want to move but he won't think of it.

Pause.

IRIS. Did you know, if Germany won the war, Hitler wanted Bridgnorth for his headquarters?

A laugh bursts out of MRS SIEVES.

MRS SIEVES. I believe you.

IRIS. I think he admired the railway links. Which, actually, is why I moved here too.

MRS SIEVES. I thought you weren't from round here.

IRIS. No, I'm from Sidcup. I don't think Hitler thought much of Sidcup. But I grew up in a house a lot like this one. My father was lame because when he was a child he walked around for six months with a broken leg.

Pause. MRS SIEVES *reconsiders* IRIS. *She looks back at the form.*

MRS SIEVES. What about if I need medicine though? / Because –

IRIS. That's free too. Is something in particular troubling you?

MRS SIEVES. It's nothing really, just. Ever since Sam come home. I didn't want to waste the sixpence, / but –

IRIS. How long have you had the trouble?

MRS SIEVES. Two years and three months.

IRIS. And what are your symptoms?

MRS SIEVES *hides her face with shame.*

MRS SIEVES. It hurts when I pass water and sometimes there's blood.

Seven

Iris's surgery. Day. IRIS *is helping a patient,* MR EAVIS *(sixties), on with his shoes, he has terrible gout.*

IRIS. See how you go with the allopurinol, and I know it's off the ration but tell your wife to lay off the Spam please, it's no good for gout. Watch you don't tread the backs down there. All right?

MR EAVIS. Thank you, doctor, goodbye.

IRIS. Goodbye.

> MR EAVIS *goes out. The buzzer sounds.*

JUDY (*off, trying to remain calm*). A Mr Blythe to see you, doctor.

> IRIS *freezes for a moment.*

IRIS. Send him in.

> JUDY *enters, followed by* GEORGE. *He looks a wreck. Exhausted, unwell.*

JUDY. This way, Mr Blythe.

IRIS. Thank you, Judy.

> JUDY *mimes excitedly behind* GEORGE, *silently mouths: 'It's the actor!'*

Thank you, Judy.

> JUDY *reluctantly exits. A pause.*

You look dreadful.

GEORGE. I'm all right. I just. I'm not sleeping well. I thought you might give me some Tuinal.

IRIS. I'll need to examine you.

GEORGE. I'm not here to play doctors and nurses.

IRIS. You're fifty-three. You're a prime candidate for a stroke or a heart attack, roll up your sleeve.

> *He sighs but takes off his jacket, rolls up his sleeve.* IRIS *straps a blood-pressure monitor round his arm. Silence. She takes his pulse as she pumps up the monitor.*
>
> *Pause.* IRIS *takes a reading, writes it down.*

GEORGE. Is it all right?

IRIS. It's a little high but nothing to worry about. Could you unbutton your shirt a little please?

> *He gives her a look, but she looks back straight-faced. He unbuttons his shirt. She puts her stethoscope on, breathes on*

it to warm it up. She places the stethoscope on his chest. He breathes.

You could have gone to any number of doctors you know.

GEORGE. I know. Do you think me very pathetic?

IRIS. No. But I wish you hadn't come.

He takes her hands.

GEORGE. I had to see you.

Pause. She pulls her hands away.

IRIS. Has *Bluebeard's Honeymoon* gone well?

GEORGE. The ending is predictable and the beard gave me a rash, but the cheques come on time, and the catering hasn't made anyone violently ill. Did you hear what I said?

IRIS. Yes, I heard.

Pause.

GEORGE. You look tired yourself. You're working too hard.

IRIS. I'm running a by-election campaign, it's rather relentless.

GEORGE. Who are you campaigning for?

IRIS. For – well, for me.

GEORGE. I'll vote for you.

IRIS. Thank you.

GEORGE. I'm not sure I have a vote, but if I do, I'll vote for you.

IRIS. George, why / have you –

GEORGE. I've found a hotel.

IRIS. No.

GEORGE. No, you're right.

IRIS. I'm not interested in being some, some *mistress*.

GEORGE. That's an ugly word to use.

IRIS. Well it's an ugly idea.

GEORGE. No it isn't. You know it isn't. Clumsy perhaps. Not ugly. Don't...

Pause.

IRIS. You know, everyone keeps telling me I look tired, and they're right. I've never been a vain woman but I look in the mirror and my face is a wartime face. I look like my mother when she was grieving my father but what is there to grieve? We won the war. We won the election. Only nobody told us victory would be so dreary. And it's your fault, actually, because it was just as dreary before, only I didn't realise it. It was perfectly tolerable, and then I met you. And the world became technicolor. And then you went again. And now I have to spend the rest of my life in black and white.

Pause.

GEORGE. I'm sorry. I'm not sure what I was thinking, I can't leave Sylvia anyway.

IRIS. She's here?

GEORGE. Yes. Since last week. It's been. Well, rather a shock for her.

IRIS. I'm sure.

GEORGE. England, I mean, and... anyway. I'll leave you in peace.

GEORGE *goes to exit.*

IRIS. I don't know what you want.

GEORGE. I want to be good. I want to be decent. I want for once in my life to be proud of myself, rather than ashamed, but I wake up thinking about you and I go to sleep thinking about you, I always thought it was a nonsense, when people talked about it like a sickness, but it is physical isn't it? It's like your skin coming off or something.

Pause. They look at each other.

IRIS. Can you get hold of a car?

Eight

Elcock kitchen. Night. LAURA, *wearing an old net curtain like a wedding veil, and her nightie, as* IRIS *cooks dinner.*

LAURA. Mummy made me go to a filthy house and she wouldn't take me to the park and then she made me eat liver for supper and I hate liver.

JULIAN. Which house is this?

IRIS. One of my patients, Mrs Sieves. I wanted her to understand the country she lives in, take that veil off please, Laura.

JULIAN. Ten's a bit young for Socialism, don't you think?

IRIS. Not at all. I said take it off!

LAURA *takes it off, sulky.*

Thank you, all right, a kiss for Daddy and up to bed please.

LAURA *kisses her father.*

LAURA. You know they're bringing Princess Elizabeth's w-wedding dress to Birmingham this weekend?

IRIS. That's marvellous. Brush your teeth, I'll be up directly.

LAURA *stomps out of the room as* IRIS *takes her apron off.*

Don't forget, I'll be away this weekend.

JULIAN. Did I know that?

IRIS. Yes, the rally in Manchester, remember? We're launching the Health Service on Sunday.

JULIAN. Oh, yes. The Trotsky jamboree.

IRIS. I'm going up a day early to review my campaign, but Helen's agreed to give Laura an outing on Saturday, she'll bring her back here after. I'll leave meals out for both of you and be back on Sunday night.

JULIAN. That's very good of Helen. Where are they going?

IRIS. She's going to take her to see the wedding dress.

JULIAN *laughs.*

JULIAN. What a secret squirrel you are! Why on earth don't you tell her?

IRIS. Because she'll be frantic with excitement all night and won't sleep a wink. I'll tell her in the morning.

Nine

Helen's cottage. LAURA *jumps up and down screaming, hysterically excited.* HELEN, *wrapped in a lurid Aztec cloak, laughs.*

LAURA. Oh thank you, Mummy! Thank you thank you thank you.

IRIS. Don't thank me, thank Helen.

LAURA *throws her arms round* HELEN.

LAURA. Thank you, Helen.

IRIS. You're a dear, I'll make it up to you.

LAURA. It's got ten thousand pearls.

HELEN. Goodness. Will no one think of the oysters?

She hands IRIS *a set of car keys.*

The clutch groans, but she goes all right. You aren't driving all the way to Manchester, surely?

IRIS. No, I'll get the train from Shrewsbury. What about you?

HELEN. Graham will drive me up in the morning. Don't forget, we've lunch with William and Hugh before the rally. Expect they want to puff you up before the by-election. I've heard Nye's speech is going to take the paint off the walls, by the way.

IRIS. We've done it, haven't we?

HELEN. We've a long way to go. This is just the beginning.

IRIS. Be good for Helen, Laura. And don't give Mrs Creevey or Daddy any trouble tonight.

She kisses LAURA *and goes.* LAURA *looks at* HELEN.

LAURA. The train is thirteen feet long. They used Chinese silkworms to make the silk. She wore the Duchess of Teck's earrings. The wedding ring was made from a nugget of Welsh gold.

HELEN. Goodness, it's going to be a long day.

Over the scene change, MARION CUTLER *broadcasts from the BBC:*

MARION. It's hard to believe that this Monday will be the much-talked-about fifth of July when the Health Service comes into force. Lately many of you have written to say 'I'm over-age', that's over-sixty, and too old to join the National Insurance. Does that mean I won't be able to get the free medical treatment and advice under the Health Service? No indeed it doesn't. It doesn't matter what your age is, whether you're married or single, whether you're rich or poor.

Ten

Hotel reception. Welsh border. IRIS *enters.* GEORGE *is waiting. She waves, shyly.*

GEORGE. Hello.

IRIS. Hello.

They are suddenly shy for a moment.

GEORGE. Good drive?

IRIS. Wonderful. I went very fast and wasn't at all afraid of crashing.

He smiles.

GEORGE. We'll have to be careful. I forgot my newspaper.

They approach the desk. Ring the bell. The MANAGER *comes out* (*Welsh, fifties*).

MANAGER. Good morning, do you have a reservation?

GEORGE *puts on an impeccable Welsh accent.*

GEORGE. Good morning, no, we don't I'm afraid, but my wife and I would like a room for the night. En suite, if you have it.

MANAGER. Yes, we've two en suites, they're rather more dear, I'm afraid.

GEORGE. That's all right. It's our seventeenth wedding anniversary.

MANAGER. Oh, how lovely. Congratulations.

IRIS. Thank you.

MANAGER. That's furniture, isn't it?

IRIS. Yes, we've gone Dutch on a new telephone table.

MANAGER. Have you stayed with us before? I'm sure your face is familiar.

GEORGE. No, but I have a twin brother, he's a travelling salesman, vacuum cleaners, he's stayed here many times and tells me your cooked breakfast is second to none.

The MANAGER *beams, flattered.*

MANAGER. Oh, well that'll be it then. Would you like a twin or a double, madam?

IRIS. Double. Please. We'd like a double.

Eleven

Hotel room. IRIS *is alone. She tries to take her wedding ring off. But it's been on her finger too long, it won't come off.* GEORGE *comes out of the bathroom.*

IRIS. I tried to take my wedding ring off. But my fingers have got so horribly fat.

GEORGE. Yes, aren't they repulsive sausages.

  GEORGE *sits beside her, kisses her fingers.*

  I've a present for you. Close your eyes.

  She closes her eyes.

  Hold out your hand.

  IRIS *holds out her hand.* GEORGE *places a banana in it. She opens her eyes. Bursts out laughing.*

IRIS. Where did you get it?

GEORGE. I've an old friend, fruit importer. I told him you were a little girl who was dying and wanted to taste one before she went.

  IRIS *peels it and starts to eat.*

IRIS. That's immoral.

GEORGE. I know, I feel awful.

  IRIS *devours the banana. When much of it has gone:*

  I really thought you were going to offer me a bite.

IRIS. Oh, do you want one?

GEORGE. No, you keep scoffing.

IRIS. I'm sorry.

GEORGE. Don't be. It's rather reassuring to glimpse that underneath you're just as disgusting as the rest of us. Do you feel guilty?

IRIS. It was my banana.

GEORGE. No. I mean...

IRIS. Oh.

,

No. I thought I would, but.

GEORGE. You don't think he'd be unfaithful?

IRIS. I think if he met someone who made him feel like this then I would want him to be. Do you? Feel guilty, I mean?

Pause.

GEORGE. You know I think English people will become much more relaxed about sex in the future.

IRIS. I don't. We tried being European during the war. I treated more cases of VD in 1946 than the rest of my career put together. Half of them cried with shame.

GEORGE. Yes, actually I've been meaning to ask you to take a look at something for me...

She laughs and hits him. He laughs too. They lie on the bed and look at one another.

IRIS. I wish I'd met you when I was young and beautiful.

GEORGE. You're very beautiful.

IRIS. I'm not young though.

GEORGE. Neither am I.

IRIS. I used to have a twenty-two-inch waist.

He props himself up on his elbow, looks at her.

What?

GEORGE. Nothing.

,

I could suddenly see how you'll look when you're a very old lady.

He kisses her. They start to make love.

Twelve

Hotel room. Later. IRIS *on the phone, in her slip.*

IRIS. I left a tray for you both in the larder, and there's a clean nightdress on her pillow, you will make sure she brushes her teeth won't you? I'm sure she just runs the tap and pretends sometimes. Did Helen say she'd behaved herself?

…

Oh good.

…

Yes everyone's very excited here.

…

Just a sandwich in my room probably.

She picks GEORGE*'s suit jacket up, folds it. Her eye is caught by the beautiful silk lining. She feels its luxury against her cheek.*

The door opens, GEORGE *is there, juggling two newspaper parcels of fish and chips and a large garment box. She puts her finger to her lips, as he creeps in.*

Mrs Creevey will be in to give you both breakfast in the morning, so don't worry about that – what's that?

…

Oh dear, well, keep the button somewhere safe, I'll sew it back on tomorrow evening.

…

Yes, goodnight.

IRIS *hangs up.* GEORGE *is on the bed, she sits, they unwrap their fish and chips.*

GEORGE. I put salt and vinegar on both, is that all right?

IRIS. Yes, thank you.

They eat in companionable silence for a while.

I expect you stay in hotels all the time, don't you?

GEORGE. Hm, quite often.

IRIS. Have you stayed at The Ritz?

GEORGE. Once. I had an interview with a lady journalist there. I came upstairs to find her lying on my bed wearing nothing but a hat.

IRIS. You mean… she / was –

GEORGE. Bare as a radish.

IRIS. No!

GEORGE. It was much harder to coax that woman out of my bed than it's ever been to coax one in.

IRIS points at herself – 'Oh, do you mean me?' He shrugs – 'I couldn't possibly comment.' They both laugh. IRIS nods at the box.

IRIS. What's that?

GEORGE. Oh. A present. I hope it's all right. I had to guess your measurements.

IRIS licks her fingers, wipes them, goes over. She picks up the box. She is stunned to see it is from Christian Dior.

IRIS. Is this –

GEORGE. It's called the New Look.

IRIS pulls out a suit. Cream jacket, black skirt. An indulgent mass of beautiful fabric.

IRIS. How did you manage / to –

GEORGE. Don't ask. Deeply criminal. Do you like it?

IRIS. It's disgusting. I love it. Thank you.

She kisses him. It turns into a yawn. They laugh.

GEORGE. Tired?

IRIS. A little.

She gets up, pulls a nightdress from her handbag. Embarrassed:

I still can't sleep naked. In case the sirens go in the middle of the night. Silly isn't it?

GEORGE. I was brought up to believe it was a carnal sin to sleep in anything but flannel pyjamas and bedsocks.

IRIS. That must be rather uncomfortable, in California.

GEORGE. In California, I'm generally…

IRIS. Bare as a radish?

GEORGE. Something like that.

She turns for the bathroom.

No, don't.

IRIS. What?

GEORGE. I want to look at you.

She laughs.

I'm serious.

She is embarrassed, but reluctantly stands there, looking anywhere but at him. Her shoulders slumped. Her posture awkward. She does not know what to do with her hands.

Slowly, under the warmth of his gaze, her posture becomes more confident. Her shoulders go back. Her spine straightens. She lifts her chin. She forgets about her hands. She feels beautiful.

She meets his gaze.

Thirteen

The next morning. GEORGE *dresses. Calls to* IRIS, *off.*

GEORGE. What train are you on?

IRIS (*offstage*). It's not till ten. Heaps of time.

GEORGE. What will we do about breakfast?

IRIS (*offstage*). I don't think we should go down, do you?

GEORGE (*Welsh*). Well I was rather looking forward to a kipper, if I'm honest.

Offstage, IRIS *laughs.*

Well? Does it fit?

IRIS (*offstage*). I think so.

IRIS *enters in the New Look suit.*

I feel like I'm wearing a birdcage. Do I look absurd?

He shakes his head.

You're rather skew-whiff, can I – ?

She comes to him, straightens his tie and collar. He watches her do it. The phone rings. They both stare at it, frozen, for a moment. GEORGE *goes to answer it.*

No, don't.

GEORGE. It's probably just the manager wanting our ration books.

GEORGE *answers.*

(*Into phone, Welsh.*) Hello?

Pause. It's not the manager. GEORGE *glances at* IRIS, *then turns his back to her.*

Yes, of course, put her through.

He waits. Then, in his own voice:

ACT TWO   105

That's all right, what is it?

…

Uh-huh. Oh dear, um…

…

No, you did the right thing. I'll be there as soon as I can.

…

I'm sorry. No, I know. I know. I'm on my way.

He hangs up.

I have to, shit, shit, where are / my –

IRIS. Here.

She hands him his shoes, watches as he pulls them on hurriedly.

Is it – what's / the –

GEORGE. I'm sorry. I'm – it's rather complicated, I wish I could –

IRIS. No, it's all right.

GEORGE. No it's not. It's not.

He takes a moment. Gathers himself.

I hope you know. How much I would like to stay here. How much I wish I were free / to –

IRIS. Well neither am I so there's no point in –

GEORGE. Why? If I were in your position –

IRIS. Well you aren't. And you never will be, it's different for men. People turn away from a divorced woman.

He takes hold of her.

GEORGE. You don't understand what this is, do you? Not properly. What you're turning away from – I don't mean me, I mean the chance to be, to be happier. It takes a lot to break up a marriage, I know that, but you're there, you're on the brink and if you don't do it now, you never will. Everything will go on just the same, and for the rest of your life. You'll survive of course, but that's what it will be, surviving, and you'll have to go through the rest of your days knowing it could have been so much better. That it could have been wonderful and not merely tolerable.

IRIS. That isn't kind, my love.

GEORGE. Kind?

IRIS. You want me to jump off a cliff but you won't hold my hand.

GEORGE. All right, well what if I did jump? What if we both did?

,

I'll tell you what would happen, you'd have to let go at the last moment. Because the second I took your hand you'd be disgusted with both of us, and I'd go sailing over the edge completely alone.

,

Well? Am I wrong?

Pause.

IRIS....

He kisses her. He leaves.

Fourteen

Elcock house. The same night. JULIAN *is sitting with* LAURA *asleep on his lap. Wilfrid Pickles on the radio.* IRIS *enters. He puts his finger to his lips – 'Shhh.'*

JULIAN. Do you remember when she was first born? This was the only way she'd sleep, little terror?

IRIS. You used to sit there for hours.

JULIAN. The blessing now is I can't feel it when my foot goes dead.

They half-laugh a doctor's black laugh together.

IRIS. I used to love reading aloud to you while you were trapped there. We got through the whole of *The Hobbit*, I think.

JULIAN. Yes and, *Varicose Veins*, by H. McPheeter. What a page-turner that was.

LAURA *shifts in her sleep a little.*

IRIS. She should be in bed. Here –

She reaches to take her.

JULIAN. Let me have just one more minute. This might be the last time it ever happens.

,

IRIS. Why?

,

JULIAN. Well, she's getting so grown-up, isn't she? How did it go in Manchester?

IRIS. Well, I think.

JULIAN. Yes, we only just got home from there ourselves.

IRIS. From Manchester?

JULIAN. Yes, I took her up on the train for the day. I wanted her to see you coming out of the conference. I thought she'd be so proud to see you. Your achievement… we stood outside the gates for hours only… well, we must have missed you.

Pause.

IRIS. What a shame. Was she very disappointed?

JULIAN. At first. Nothing a camel ride couldn't fix. Whoever thought to have a political rally in a pleasure garden?

IRIS *takes off her coat. He sees her new clothes.*

Hullo.

IRIS. Oh. Yes, it's new.

> LAURA *wakes. She sees* IRIS. *Gasps. The sight of her mother is so spectacular, she's not sure she is not still dreaming.*

LAURA. Mummy. You look wonderful.

IRIS. Thank you.

LAURA. You look like Princess Margaret.

IRIS. And you should be in bed, come on, chop-chop.

> LAURA *clambers off* JULIAN, IRIS *ushers her out. While she is gone,* JULIAN *crumples. He covers his face. Tries to smother his grief.* IRIS *returns, she has taken her New Look jacket off and put a cardigan on. He gathers himself.*

JULIAN. Whatever you think you need to say, I don't need to hear it.

IRIS. Julian.

JULIAN. I don't want to know, Iris.

IRIS. I've fallen in love.

JULIAN. No.

IRIS. I'd like a divorce.

> JULIAN *stares at the floor, shakes his head. She kneels beside him, takes his hand.*

I've fallen in love.

> *Very suddenly, he smacks her across the face. She falls. She puts her hand to her eye, blood on her fingers.* JULIAN *is immediately horrified, scrambles to her.*

JULIAN. Iris, I'm sorry – God, I'm sorry – are you – oh my God –

> *He tries to examine her face. Suddenly she flies back at him, raining slaps and blows, uncontrollable rage and grief. They fight an ugly, vicious scrap on the floor, until they are breathless, exhausted.*

Stop it – stop it! Let me look at your eye, you silly woman!

She falls still. Lets him examine her eye, which he does with skill and tenderness.

There's a lot of blood, but it's not actually that deep.

IRIS. I think your wedding ring caught me.

JULIAN. Yes. Sorry.

,

Who is he then?

Pause.

All right. I wouldn't answer that either.

Pause. He finds a handkerchief, gently cleans her wound.

I almost had someone for a bit. While I was away.

IRIS. Who? A WREN?

He makes a small non-committal sound.

JULIAN. I wish I could be chivalrous but I can't cop to cruelty or adultery. All my female patients will leave me.

IRIS. No, of course. Could I desert you?

JULIAN. Up to you. Your life will be ruined either way. Laura's too. I'm not trying to be unkind. But no one is going to vote for a divorced woman, you know that, don't you?

IRIS. Mavis Tate was an MP and she was divorced twice.

JULIAN. Yes and then she put her head in an oven. Have you any idea what kind of existence you're leaping into?

IRIS. I don't know. I don't…

I keep trying to imagine it and I can't.

Pause.

JULIAN. You know I know two different men who came home from the war and murdered their wives. I'm not joking, murdered them. I thought I was doing rather well in comparison.

He laughs, humourless.

Do you think I'm evil?

IRIS. Oh, don't be / silly.

JULIAN. I'm serious. He called me evil.

IRIS. Who?

JULIAN. Your chum. Bevan. He said the selling of medical practices was evil.

IRIS. *An* evil.

JULIAN. What?

IRIS. He said 'an evil', not evil.

JULIAN. Well if you must split / hairs then –

IRIS. I just think they're rather / different if you –

JULIAN. Do you think I'm evil?

Pause.

Goodness what a long pause.

IRIS. No, of course I don't think you're evil.

She touches his face. He pulls her close. They hold each other. Pause.

JULIAN. It'll never be enough you know.

IRIS. What?

JULIAN. This… the Health Service. I don't doubt it'll start beautifully. But the human body can go wrong in so many ways. And people take for granted anything they get for free you know, they can't help it. They abuse it. The beautiful girlfriend whose attentions you were once so grateful for will become the tired wife who keeps you waiting too long for your supper. There'll never be enough money. Never enough beds, nurses… wheelchairs, what-have-you. The whole thing's bound to capsize eventually.

IRIS. Perhaps. But then the idea won't have failed. We will have failed the idea.

Pause.

JULIAN. Are you sure the cornea's all right? Follow my finger.

He holds up his index finger, moves it from side to side, IRIS *follows it with her eyes.*

Fifteen

Howells house. MRS HOWELLS *has just answered the door to* IRIS.

MRS HOWELLS. Sorry. He's out.

But IRIS *shoves past her, pushes into the house.*

IRIS. I need to see him.

MRS HOWELLS. Excuse me. I've told you plainly, / he isn't here – excuse me!

IRIS. Where is he?

MRS HOWELLS. He's got to do right by her. For better or worse. / That's marriage.

SYLVIA *enters.*

IRIS. George? Are you –

IRIS *is arrested by the sight of* SYLVIA. *Just out of the bath, a towel round her, dripping water. She suffers from aphasia. She looks nothing like the glamorous woman we've seen. She's suffered a severe stroke. Her hair is growing out from being shaved. She is frightened of* IRIS.

SYLVIA. Certain saddles? Go and guy! Go and guy! [Who is she? Go away! Go away!]

IRIS. Sorry, / I'm… my name is Doctor Elcock.

MRS HOWELLS. No, luvvy, you get back there, you'll catch your death.

SYLVIA. Never on the heigh-ho? [Why is she here?]

IRIS. I'm Doctor Elcock. I was –

SYLVIA. Dolly? [Doctor?]

IRIS. Sorry?

MRS HOWELLS. All right, that's enough, / come on –

SYLVIA shakes MRS HOWELLS' *guiding hands off roughly.*

SYLVIA. How dolly? [You're a doctor?]

IRIS. I'm so sorry, is – is Mr Blythe here?

SYLVIA. Godge? Godge!

GEORGE (*offstage*). Darling, what are you doing? There's water everywhere.

GEORGE enters, sleeves rolled up, holding SYLVIA's *dressing gown. He sees* IRIS.

Oh.

MRS HOWELLS. She just barged in.

SYLVIA (*points to* IRIS). Dolly? [Doctor?]

GEORGE. Yes. Yes, she's a doctor, uh… this is my wife, Sylvia. Sylvia, this is Doctor Elcock. You needn't be frightened.

IRIS *nods.* SYLVIA *relaxes a little but is still wary, on edge.*

SYLVIA. Soap driver is the sooty swatch never tests? [Why didn't you tell me we were having guests?]

GEORGE. Doctor Elcock is Mum's doctor. Isn't that right, Queenie?

He looks at MRS HOWELLS.

MRS HOWELLS. That's right, dear.

SYLVIA. Snap pocket while the kiddy goes! Lily list and and and bracket tight! [Well I just wasn't ready for visitors! I look a a a complete fright!]

GEORGE. You look just fine, darling.

ACT TWO 113

SYLVIA. I'll jake my diddle! [No I don't!]

SYLVIA *starts searching for her handbag.*

Cookie well… uh, digger space hm? Some, some liquor cherry? [Just let me put my face on. Where's my handbag?]

GEORGE. What is it? Your dressing gown? Here –

SYLVIA. Liquor cherry! [No! My lipstick!]

GEORGE. Your… handbag? Is that – ? Handbag?

She nods. He finds it. Gives it to her. SYLVIA *takes out a lipstick. Gives him her compact.*

SYLVIA. Godge, will it glimmer. [George, hold the mirror.]

GEORGE *understands, holds the mirror open for her. She attempts to apply the lipstick but she has right-side weakness in her dominant hand, so she guides it with her left hand. Even so, her movements are imprecise.*

GEORGE. Let me help you –

But SYLVIA *jerks away from him, laughs.*

SYLVIA. Nice and find it!! [I can do it!!]

But she can't. Her hand shakes uncontrollably. IRIS *watches.* GEORGE *cannot. This continues almost as long as feels unbearable.*

Suddenly IRIS *goes to her, takes the lipstick with a doctor's gentle but unassailable authority, tilts* SYLVIA*'s chin and carefully, precisely applies the lipstick.*

When she has finished, she takes the compact from GEORGE, *shows* SYLVIA *her reflection.* SYLVIA *nods, pleased.*

Celery. [Thank you.]

She fleetingly strikes a movie-star pose, making fun of herself. Then she wilts, suddenly starts to fall. GEORGE *catches her.*

GEORGE. Whoops-a-daisy.

SYLVIA. Godge... Godge...

She clings to him.

GEORGE. It's all right. You're all right.

SYLVIA. Biggit willow, darling. Uh, um, jump slipper now does it, does it hiding. [I'm sorry, darling. I suddenly feel very, very tired.]

GEORGE. You look tired. Why don't you get into bed?

SYLVIA *gestures to* IRIS.

SYLVIA. Is it window, is it special on the layaway? [Can you tell her I'm sorry, I'm not very well just at present?]

GEORGE. I think she wants to – she's apologising, she isn't very well.

SYLVIA. Bucket sucker pat. [But I'll be better soon.]

GEORGE. But she'll be better soon.

SYLVIA. No butter with the, uh, butter to the berry will you, dolly? How lashing, party? [You won't go round telling everyone, will you, doctor? I can trust you, can't I?]

GEORGE. She doesn't want you to tell anyone you saw her like this.

IRIS. No, of course.

SYLVIA. Tickle! [Promise!]

GEORGE. What?

SYLVIA. Tickle!

GEORGE. I think she, um, I think she wants you to promise, is that right?

SYLVIA *nods.*

IRIS. Oh. Yes. I promise.

MRS HOWELLS. Come on, luvvy, let Queenie get you to bed.

MRS HOWELLS *guides* SYLVIA *out.* IRIS *and* GEORGE *stand in silence, not meeting each others' eyes. Eventually:*

IRIS. What is it, a stroke?

He nods.

She's so young.

GEORGE. Yes, it was very bad luck.

She hopes to go back to work and she doesn't want the studios to write her off as a cripple.

IRIS. But she's – I mean, that's never going to –

GEORGE. I know. But I don't think it hurts to let her hope. She's been in a sanatorium back home, only the money's going out faster than I can earn it. I've found a specialist in London who'll treat her on the Health Service so –

IRIS. So you brought her here.

GEORGE. Yes.

IRIS. And you'll go to London.

GEORGE. Yes.

IRIS. Together.

GEORGE. Yes.

Pause.

Perhaps one day, when she's better…

IRIS. Yes. When she's better.

They both know she will never be better. GEORGE *sits, crumples, exhausted himself.*

GEORGE. Still, bit of a mess, eh? The only thing that makes it bearable is you'd never have left him anyway. Would you.

?

Or would you?

IRIS. No. That's what I wanted to tell you. I've – Julian and I, we've managed to patch things up.

GEORGE. Oh.

IRIS. Yes, he came to meet me in Manchester today and he and Laura and I had such a lovely time, you know, camel rides and well everything just felt jolly for once, and we had a good talk, very honest. He's agreed to see the consultant again, and, we're going to have a holiday, after the election. Maybe the Via Alpina, have you ever been?

GEORGE. No, I…

IRIS. Oh, you must go, really, the views are breathtaking, / no honestly, they really are.

GEORGE. Why did you come here? Iris?

IRIS. What?

GEORGE. Why did you come here?

IRIS. Oh, just to tell you. I'll be all right. We've had a nice time haven't we, but it wouldn't have worked anyway, you see. You can go off to London and not think about me for another second. I'm very grateful for everything you've done to help me but we must both look to the future now.

,

GEORGE. God you really do sound like a politician.

IRIS. Thank you.

,

GEORGE. Iris, where have you gone?

He reaches for her.

SYLVIA (*offstage*). Godge?

Pause. The tiniest movement in IRIS*'s hand. But she does not meet his action.*

IRIS. Your wife wants you.

GEORGE. Yes. All right, well. Goodbye.

IRIS. Goodbye.

He exits. The minute he has gone, IRIS *dissolves. She silently sobs into her hands.*

A moment, then MRS HOWELLS *enters.* IRIS *immediately pulls herself together.*

MRS HOWELLS. Oh. I thought you'd left.

IRIS *swallows her grief, sticks her chin out, stares back at her.*

IRIS. Yes, I'm going now. I hope I can rely on your vote.

IRIS *marches out. The sound of a train approaching grows louder and louder.*

Sixteen

Iris's surgery. Monday morning. 5th July. IRIS *is asleep in her clothes on the examining table.* AVERILL HUGHES (*thirty-two, Jamaican, district nurse's uniform*), *sits beside her, reading* Picturegoer. IRIS *stirs.* AVERILL *puts her magazine down.*

AVERILL. Here she is. Don't move.

IRIS *sits up. Immediately regrets it.*

Told you. You had a bang to your head. You got a headache?

IRIS. No.

AVERILL. Your neck hurting?

IRIS. No.

AVERILL. You feel sick?

IRIS. No.

AVERILL. Little bit confused / maybe?

IRIS. No, I'm –

AVERILL. Tired?

,

IRIS. Yes. Quite tired.

AVERILL. Oh well. That's how the body tells you you're doing too much.

IRIS *stares at her.*

We had ourselves quite a chat last night.

IRIS. I'm so sorry. I can't, uh.

AVERILL. District Nurse Averill Hughes. The bedpan queen. They call me to take you home only you didn't want to go.

IRIS. Who?

AVERILL. The people who found you.

,

At the train station.

Pause.

IRIS. Oh yes, of course. I tripped, didn't I?

AVERILL. Uh-huh. Seem so.

IRIS *looks at the bandage round her hand.*

IRIS. Where's Judy?

AVERILL. I don't know who that is.

IRIS. My receptionist.

AVERILL. Oh. Not here yet. It's only twenty-past eight. You want to wash your face?

IRIS. No, / I'm –

AVERILL. Wash your face. You don't want to scare your patients.

She gets a wet flannel, gives it to IRIS. IRIS *stares at it.*

Go on.

IRIS *washes her face.* AVERILL *shows her the article she was reading.*

I love Stanley Holloway.

IRIS. I don't know him.

ACT TWO 119

AVERILL. He's a supporting player, that why. Not leading man. Look at that face. Handsome . You know *The Lion and Albert*? I know it off by heart. The whole thing. I've seen it ten times in the cinema. Bought my ticket for the boat there too. Tropic Theatre. Kingston, Jamaica. Back home we stand up for the National Anthem at the start of the film. You don't do that here. Embarrassed meself at the Odeon.

IRIS. Why did you come here?

AVERILL. You call and we came. I want to help the Motherland.

IRIS. No, I mean. Shropshire.

AVERILL. Oh. My husband Jellicoe was RAF during the war. He flew Spitfires. Him… he's buried in St Mary Magdalene.

IRIS. Oh. I'm sorry.

AVERILL. I always said, I'd follow that man to the end of the earth. And the end of the earth turn out to be somewhere near Kidderminster. You got a crack in your ceiling.

IRIS. I know.

AVERILL. Poor old Motherland. She a very tired mother, you ask me. Still, you can't be everything to everybody. You want coffee?

IRIS. You don't have to make me coffee.

AVERILL. To be honest I was hinting for you to make me one.

IRIS. Oh. Yes, of / course –

HELEN *blasts into the room.*

HELEN. You little *idiot*.

AVERILL. Excuse me –

HELEN. You silly little fathead!

AVERILL. You need to wait in the waiting room!

HELEN. Who are you?

AVERILL. I'm Ginger Rogers, who are you?

IRIS (*to* AVERILL). It's all right. / She's a friend – Helen, calm down –

HELEN. This close, *this close*, and you try to capsize the whole thing good Lord what are you wearing?

IRIS. It's new.

HELEN. It's obscene.

AVERILL. I leave you to it.

> AVERILL *takes out a notebook, writes.*

My telephone number at the hospital. In case you ever want to catch the train again.

> *She rips out the page, gives it to* IRIS. AVERILL *goes.* HELEN *takes in the room.*

HELEN. Did you *sleep* here?

> IRIS *puts her shoes on, doesn't answer.*

God, this is like some dreadful play, some dreadful bloody melodrama. All right, don't worry. We'll stop by the house, you can patch it up with Julian, then go straight on to the station –

IRIS. Where are we going?

HELEN. Party HQ.

IRIS. I can't go to London.

HELEN. Well you're going. They want to see you, you've spooked them. The most desiccated men in Britain and you've made them damp with anxiety, it's almost impressive.

IRIS. What are they anxious about?

HELEN. Oh, I don't know, that you've gone completely mad? That you missed the rally to launch the Health Service we've sweated blood over? That you've deserted your war-hero husband weeks before a by-election?

IRIS. How do they know?

HELEN. Because you missed lunch yesterday, so William rang your house first thing this morning and Julian told him the whole wretched saga! They sent me to slap some sense into you and I found Laura at the kitchen table looking completely lost while Julian tried to cook porridge in a fish kettle. Come on, powder your nose, we can make the nine-thirty if we hurry.

IRIS. I'm not going, Helen.

HELEN. It's not a fucking invitation, Iris.

IRIS. It's the first day of the Health Service.

HELEN. Well, you're not a GP now, you're an MP, or at least you will be if we can sort this bloody mess out.

IRIS. I can't fight the seat.

HELEN. Don't talk rot.

IRIS. They won't vote for a divorced woman.

HELEN. You're not getting divorced. I forbid it. And anyway, Mavis Tate was divorced twice.

IRIS. Mavis Tate's constituency wasn't full of Catholics.

HELEN. All right, Nancy Astor.

IRIS. Also Conservative.

HELEN. So?

IRIS. So you can do what you like if you're a Tory, you can go to bed with a bloody Springer Spaniel if you're a Tory, and anyway they were both married again by the time they went to the polls.

HELEN. I still think you've got a chance, / half a chance, if you'd just –

IRIS. Why are you pretending to be stupid?

HELEN. I wasn't aware I was pretending.

IRIS. If I fight this election, you know what the story will be, you just *told* me the story, the story will be hypocrite Socialist abandons war-wounded husband, left-wing termagant smashes up home, now watch her smash up the country, that's what the story will be, and would you vote for that woman? Honestly? Because I bloody wouldn't!

HELEN *stares at her. Disappointment. Disbelief.*

HELEN. What's wrong with you? Why can't you just keep your feelings locked up like a normal person!

IRIS. Are you very angry?

HELEN. OF COURSE I'M BLOODY ANGRY! YOU'VE BROKEN MY HEART!

Pause.

IRIS. I'm sorry I missed the rally. How did it go?

HELEN. Oh, a disaster. Nye called the Tories vermin. He used the actual word, vermin. In the moment of our greatest triumph, he made himself look a bitter little prig and they'll never let us forget it. Not the Party, not the voters. The British tolerate incest more comfortably than they tolerate bad manners, and now the Health Service has been used to humiliate them, what reason have the Tories to be loyal to it? What's to stop them hacking away at it every chance they get?

IRIS. Nye was never going to share the heroics.

HELEN. Well it's unforgivable! It's unforgivable! He's turned our greatest moment of civilisation into a bloody pissing contest!

,

IRIS. How did Laura seem, when you saw her?

HELEN. See for yourself, she's in the waiting room –

IRIS. Laura's here? Laura! Why did you bring her here? I'm not ready to –

LAURA *enters.*

Darling. What a nice surprise!

LAURA *holds out the brochure from the wedding-dress exhibition.*

LAURA. I brought you the souvenir brochure. You didn't get to see it last night.

ACT TWO 123

IRIS. Goodness how lovely. Darling, I need to explain / something, and it's going to be quite difficult for you to understand, but –

HELEN. Don't. The minute you tell her, that's it, it's real, and you won't be able to undo it, Iris, so stop, just stop for a / moment and –

IRIS. Say goodbye to Helen.

LAURA. Goodbye, Helen.

HELEN. This was it, you know. This was the window.

HELEN exhales, and leaves. LAURA is looking through the brochure.

IRIS. Laura? Laura, darling, are you listening to me?

LAURA. Uh-huh, look at that, Mama.

She shows her an image of the wedding dress. IRIS tosses the brochure aside.

IRIS. Laura, do you know how many extra clothing coupons the Princess was given by the government to acquire that dress? Two hundred. Do you know who else got given extra coupons to buy a wedding dress?

LAURA. Um...

IRIS. No one. No one else in the entire country, do you think that's fair?

LAURA. I don't know. Does it matter?

Pause.

IRIS. No. No, it doesn't matter. I'm sorry.

She picks the brochure up, smooths it out, gives it to LAURA.

Here. Laura, Mummy and Daddy aren't going to live together any more. So you and I will be on our own rather a lot, just us, all right?

LAURA. Like during the war?

IRIS. Exactly, like during the war, only better, because you'll still be able to see Daddy lots and lots.

Pause.

LAURA. Are you going to be divorced?

IRIS. Yes.

Pause.

LAURA. Like Charlie Chaplin?

IRIS. Yes. I'm sorry, darling, I know this must be –

She tries to pull LAURA *to her but* LAURA *pushes her away.* LAURA *stares at the floor for a few moments.* IRIS *watches her but gives her space.*

LAURA. Are we going to London?

IRIS. No, Mummy won't be going to London any more.

LAURA. But… because… where will we live?

IRIS. I think in a flat, probably.

LAURA. I like flats.

IRIS. Do you?

LAURA. Yes, I think stairs are overrated, can it have blue curtains?

IRIS. Definitely.

LAURA. Can it have a television?

IRIS. I'm not sure.

LAURA. Let's pretend it can.

IRIS. All right. It can have a television, and a refrigerator, and on Saturdays we can stay in bed and read comics all morning.

LAURA. And then go to the pictures.

IRIS. And then go to the pictures.

LAURA. And see cowboys and Indians.

IRIS. All right.

LAURA. I like the Indians.

IRIS. Good for you.

JUDY enters. She's surprised to see IRIS here already.

JUDY. Oh. Morning, Doctor Elcock.

IRIS. Good morning, Judy.

JUDY takes in the room, IRIS's bag. She whispers to IRIS, mindful of LAURA.

JUDY. I have such dreadful fights with Richard sometimes. I slept in the bath once I was so cross with him, only he never noticed so the joke was on me. Our tap drips. (*Louder.*) I hope it's all right, I opened the doors, there's ever so many people outside.

IRIS. All right. Off we go.

IRIS is overwhelmed for a moment with terror and vertigo. She tries to conceal it from LAURA, swallow it. Forces a smile. She finds her white coat, puts it on over her New Look clothes. Her fingers fumble the buttons.

LAURA. Do you want help?

IRIS desperately tries not to cry.

IRIS. Yes please.

LAURA does the buttons up for her.

LAURA. That's better.

IRIS stands, broken, hunched, exhausted.

It'll be all right I think.

IRIS. Do you?

LAURA. I think so. Probably. I don't know. Here.

She puts a stethoscope around IRIS's neck. Picks up the souvenir brochure.

I'm going to put this in the waiting room. In case any of your patients want to read it.

IRIS. Thank you. That's very thoughtful.

LAURA *exits.* IRIS *collapses for a moment. Then gathers herself.* JUDY *enters.*

JUDY. Ready for your first patient, Doctor Elcock?

IRIS. Yes, thank you, Judy.

IRIS *stands up straight. Takes a deep breath. The theatre becomes the waiting room.*

IRIS *addresses the audience.*

Now. What seems to be the problem?

The End.

www.nickhernbooks.co.uk

facebook.com/nickhernbooks

twitter.com/nickhernbooks